Mergers in the Global Markets

Felix I. Lessambo

Mergers in the Global Markets

A Comparative Approach to the Competition and National Security Laws among the US, EU, and China

palgrave macmillan

Felix I. Lessambo
School of Business
Central Connecticut State University
New Britain, CT, USA

ISBN 978-3-030-43557-8 ISBN 978-3-030-43558-5 (eBook)
https://doi.org/10.1007/978-3-030-43558-5

This Palgrave Macmillan imprint is published by the registered company Springer Nature Switzerland AG
The registered company address is: Gewerbestrasse 11, 6330 Cham, Switzerland

Acknowledgements

Writing a book is always a challenge. But writing a book on Mergers in Global Markets, geared to Executives and MBAs, a more daring intellectual exercise.

I would like to thank my astoundingly supportive friends who motivated me all along the project, knowing my dedication to the subject and thought I am more than able to complete this project: Dr. Marsha Gordon, Dr. Lavern A. Wright, Dr. Lester Reid, Reverend Jonathan Samminga, and Jerry Izouele.

And last but not least, thank you to all the original readers of this book when it was in its infancy. Without your enthusiasm and encouragement, this book may have never been ready.

Contents

Abbreviations

AML	Anti-Monopoly Law (China)
APA	Administrative Procedure Act
CFI (EU)	Court of First Instance
CFIUS	Committee on Foreign Investment in the United States
DoJ	Department of Justice (USA)
EU	European Union
EUMR	European Union Mergers Regulations
FINSA	Foreign Investment and National Security Act
FIRRMA	The Foreign Investment Risk Review Modernization Act
FRAND	Fair, Reasonable, and Non-Discriminatory
FTC	Federal Trade Commission
HHI	Herfindahl–Hirschmann Index
IEEPA	International Emergency Economic Powers Act
IJV	International Joint Venture
LBO	Leveraged Buyout
M&A	Mergers and Acquisitions
MOFCOM	Ministry of Commerce (China)
NDRC	National Development and Reform Commission (China)
SAIC	State Administration for Industry and Commerce
SAMR	State Administration for Market Regulation (China)
SEP	Standard-Essential Patent
TFEU	Treaty on the Functioning of the European Union

List of Figures

List of Cited Cases

- The US
  - Am. Banana v. United Fruit Co., 213 U.S. 347 (1909).
  - Brown Shoe Co. v. United States, 370 U.S. 294, 330 (1962).
  - City of Lafayette v. La. Power & Light Co., 435 U.S. 389, 398 (1978).
  - F. Hoffmann-LaRoche Ltd. v. Empagran S.A., 542 U.S. 155, 164 (2004).
  - McElderry v. Cathay Pacific, 678 F Suppl.
  - McGlinch v. Shell Chemical Co., 845 F.2d 802, 812—13 (9th Cir. 1988).
  - Motorola Mobility LLC v. AU Optronics Corp., 775 F.3d 816 (7th Cir.), cert. denied, 135 S. Ct. 2837 (2015).
  - Nat'l Soc. of Prof'l Eng'rs v. United States, 435 U.S. 679 (1978).
  - Phillips Petroleum Co. v. Heeremac, No. H-98-1698 (S.D. Tex. Jan. 22, 1999).
  - Ralls Corp. v. Comm. on Foreign Inv., 758 F.3d 296, 301 (D.C. Cir. 2014).
  - Reiter v. Sonotone Corp., 442 U.S. 330, 343 (1979).
  - Standard Oil Co. v. FTC, 340 U.S. 231, 248–49 (1951).
  - Timberlane Lumber Co. v. Bank of America, 549 F.2d 1287 (3d Cir. 1979).
  - United States v. Aluminium Co. of America, 148 F.2d 416, 444 (2d Cir. 1945).

- US SC 442 US 86, 131 n.1 (1975).
- United States vs. Baker Hughes, 908 F.2d 981, at 984.
- U.S. v Philadelphia National Bank, 374 U.S. 321 (1963).
- U.S. v. Marine Bancorporation, 418 U.S. 602 (1974).

• The EU
  - Case COMP/M.6850 Marine Harvest/Morpol.
  - Case T-704/14 Marine Harvest v Commission.
  - Case T-102/96, Gencor Ltd. v. Comm'n, 1999 E.C.R. II-753, 761–62.
  - Case COMP/M.1858 Thomson-CSF/Racal(II).
  - Case COMP/M.5932 News Corp/BskyB.
  - Case COMP/M.759 Sun Alliance/Royal Insurance.
  - Case COMP/M.567 Lyonnaise des Eaux/Northumbrian Water.
  - Case COMP/M.1346 EDF/London Electricity.
  - Commission Decision IV/M.1069 – WorldCom/MCI, 1999 O.J. (L 116) 1 (EC).
  - Commission Decision COMP/M.1741 – MCI WorldCom/Sprint, 2000 O.J. (L 300) 1 (EC).
  - Commission Decision COMP/M.2220 – General Electric/Honeywell, 2001 O.J. (L 48) 1 (EC).
  - Cases COMP/34.579 – MasterCard, COMP/36.518 – EuroCommerce and COMP/38.580 – Commercial Cards, Decision C (2007)6474 final of 19 December 2007, upheld on appeal by the General Court on 24 May 2012 in Case T-111/08 MasterCard [2012] ECR II-not yet reported.

• China
  - The GE Shenhua Case.
  - The Huawei v. InterDigital Case.
  - The Mercedes-Benz and Dongfeng-Nissan Case.
  - The Qualcomm Case.
  - The Microsoft Case.
  - The Tetra Park Case.
  - The Savio Machine Tessili S.P.A Case.
  - The Seagate/Samsung Case.
  - The Silvinit/Uralkali Case.

PART I

Mergers and Acquisitions Policies and Approaches

CHAPTER 1

Overview of Mergers and Acquisitions

1.1 General

In 2017, about 15,000 merger and acquisition deals were announced in the United States, representing about $2 trillion in total value.[1] Business expansion occurs mainly through mergers and acquisitions. Mergers are one means by which firms can improve their ability to compete.[2] According to information collected by the leading M&A database Zephyr, global markets announced 89,440 global deals worth $6.1 trillion. Globally, the United States, China, the UK, Ireland, the Netherlands, Hong Kong, and Australia received the most M&A activity. US targets topped the rankings by both volume and value in 2015. In all 14,357 deals worth USD 1,942,778 million were announced over the 12 months.[3] Top two deals boost M&A value: (i) the Pfizer's agreement to acquire Irish pharmaceuticals maker Allergan for USD 160,000 million[4] and (ii) the Anheuser-Busch InBev's USD 131,730 million acquisition of UK-based beer manufacturer SABMiller, to create a brewing giant that

[1] Carl Shapiro (2019): Protecting Competition in the American Economy: Merger Control, Tech Titans, Labor Markets, *Journal of Economic Perspectives*, Vol. 33, No. 3, Summer 2019, p. 72.

[2] Deborah P. Majoras (2001): GE-Honeywell: The US Decision, Antitrust Law Section State Bar of Georgia, p. 3.

[3] Zephyr Annual M&A Activity Report Global, FY 2015, p. 3.

[4] This deal is subject to regulatory and shareholder approval and is expected to complete in mid-2016.

F. I. Lessambo, *Mergers in the Global Markets*,
https://doi.org/10.1007/978-3-030-43558-5_1

would produce about a third of all beer consumed globally.[5] Despite the differences in purposes, objectives, and policies, mergers and acquisitions review process presents similarities in the three main economic blocks.

All the three major markets—United States, EU, and China—subject cross-mergers to their competition and national security reviews. The purposes of competition review seem broadly identical, while the stated purposes of the national security introduced respectively a perceived hypocrisy of protectionism.

> The reference to domestic enterprises related to national security in a broad range of areas clearly provides an opportunity for government authorities to reject, on security grounds, a transaction which would be otherwise be permissible (or even encouraged) under the Foreign Investment Industries Catalog.[6]

The vagueness of the concept of "national security" provides discretion in assessing and deciding on foreign investment attempts by foreign businesses.

1.2 Methods of Business Combination

A business combination is a transaction in which the acquirer obtains control of another business (the acquiree). Business combinations are a common way for companies to grow in size, rather than growing through organic (internal) activities. There are several methods for achieving a business combination.

- Acquisition

An acquisition usually refers to the purchase of one corporation by another, through either the purchase of its shares, or the purchase of its assets. That is, an acquisition can take the form of a purchase of the stock or other equity interests of the target entity, or the acquisition of all or a substantial amount of its assets. In a share purchase the buyer buys the shares of the target company from the shareholders of the target company.

[5] Zephyr Annual M&A Activity Report Global, FY 2015, p. 20.

[6] Vivienne Bath (2013): National Security and Chinese Investment Policy, *Harvard Business Law Review* (online), Vol. 3, p. 85.

The buyer then takes on the company with all its assets and liabilities. However, in an asset purchase the buyer buys the assets of the target company from the target company. In simplest form this leaves the target company as an empty shell, and the cash it receives from the acquisition is then paid back to its shareholders by dividend or through liquidation. One of the advantages of an asset purchase for the buyer is that it can "cherry-pick" the assets that it wants and leave the assets—and liabilities—that it does not.

- Merger

A merger is a corporate strategy of combining different companies into a single company in order to enhance the financial and operational strengths of both organizations. In a merger, two separate companies combine and only one of them survives. In other words, the merged (acquired) company goes out of existence, leaving its assets and liabilities to the acquiring company. The three main types of mergers are: (i) horizontal mergers which increase market share, (ii) vertical mergers which exploit existing synergies, and (iii) concentric mergers which expand the product offering.

- Consolidation

A consolidation or amalgamation is the merger and acquisition of many smaller companies into a few much larger ones. Shares of the new company are exchanged for shares of the merging ones. Two similarly sized companies usually consolidate rather than merge. Although the distinction between merger and consolidation is important, the terms are often used interchangeably, with either used to refer generally to a joining of the assets and liabilities of two companies. In general, the consolidation process allows a business to rethink their functions and systems in a more efficient way in order to reduce the operating costs. For instance, the acquisition of goods and services can be centralized, which helps the merged company adopt a corporate-wide pricing policy.

- Leveraged buyout

A leveraged buyout (LBO) is a type of acquisition that occurs when a group of investors, sometimes led by the management of a company (management buyout or MBO), borrows funds to purchase the company. Put differently, a LBO is the acquisition of another company using a significant amount of borrowed money to meet the cost of acquisition. The assets of the company being acquired are often used as collateral for the loans, along with the assets of the acquiring company. The assets and future earnings of the company are used to secure the financing required to purchase the company. Sometimes employees are allowed to participate through an employee stock ownership plan, which may provide tax advantages and improve employee productivity by giving employees an equity stake in the company.

- Holding company

A holding company is a company that owns sufficient voting stock to have a controlling interest in one or more companies called subsidiaries. Effective working control or substantial influence can be gained through ownership of as little as 5 percent to as much as 51 percent of the outstanding shares, depending on how widely the shares are distributed. A holding company that engages in the management of the subsidiaries is called a parent company. A holding company usually does not produce goods or services itself; rather, its purpose is to own shares of other companies to form a corporate group.

- Divestitures

A divestiture involves the sale of a portion of a company. Two popular means of divestiture are spin-offs and equity carve-outs. The injunction of divestiture is very often the remedy chosen to resolve competition problems arising from mergers and acquisitions. For instance, in the Ciba-Geigy case, the purpose of the divestiture of the Sandoz Corn Herbicide Business was to ensure the continuation of the Sandoz Corn Herbicide Business as an ongoing, viable enterprise engaged in the research, development, manufacture, distribution, and sale of corn herbicides independent of Ciba, Sandoz, and Novartis and able to compete with Ciba, Sandoz, and Novartis and to remedy the lessening of competition alleged in the Commission's complaint.[7]

- Hostile versus Friendly combinations

Acquisitions can either be hostile or friendly. In a hostile acquisition, the acquiring, or bidder, company makes an offer to purchase the acquired or target company, but the management of the target company resists the offer. At that point, the bidder often tries to take control of the target through a tender offer, whereby the bidder offers to purchase a majority of the target's stock at a predetermined price, set sufficiently higher than the current market price to attract the shareholders' attention. Hostile acquisitions are typically more expensive for both parties since they involve more time and negotiations, fees to experts such as attorneys and investment bankers, and may result in a bidding war where multiple bidders enter the contest for control. The large number of hostile acquisitions in the 1980s led to the coining of the term "market for corporate control." This terminology reflects the view that acquisitions are really market-based contests whereby corporate managers bid to control corporate assets, with the highest bidder receiving control. Though hostile acquisitions receive much of the media attention surrounding acquisitions, the great majority of acquisitions are friendly. In a friendly acquisition, the management of both companies come to an agreement over the terms of the acquisition. Many acquisitions that begin as hostile end up being completed on a friendly basis.

1.3 Motives for Acquisitions

The overriding motive for any acquisition should be to maximize shareholder value. There has been increasing emphasis on maximizing shareholder value and managers are under more and more pressure to do so. The threat of a hostile takeover places pressure on all corporate managers to manage their companies to maximize value, or risk being taken over and restructured by another management. Increasingly competitive global capital markets, active institutional investors, active and independent boards of directors, and better informed market participants have all

[7] FTC v. Ciba-Geigy et al.

led to an increased focus by shareholders on shareholder value, and have placed increased pressure on corporate managers to maximize shareholder value. Acquisitions are a means of creating shareholder value by exploiting synergies, increasing growth, replacing inefficient managers, gaining market power, and extracting benefits from financial and operational restructuring. However, for value to be created, the benefits of these motives must exceed the costs.

These motives are considered to add shareholder value:

- Economies of scale: This refers to the fact that the combined company can often reduce duplicate departments or operations, lowering the costs of the company relative to theoretically the same revenue stream, thus increasing profit.
- Increased revenue/Increased market share: This motive assumes that the company will be absorbing a major competitor and its power (by capturing increased market share) to set prices.
- Cross-selling: For example, a bank buying a stockbroker could then sell its banking products to the stockbroker's customers, while the broker can sign up the bank's customers for brokerage accounts. Or, a manufacturer can acquire and sell complementary products.
- Synergy: Better use of complementary resources.
- Taxes: A profitable company can buy a loss maker to use the target's tax write-offs. In the United States and many other countries, rules are in place to limit the ability of profitable companies to "shop" for loss-making companies, limiting the tax motive of an acquiring company.
- Geographical or other diversification: This is designed to smooth the earnings results of a company, which over the long term smoothens the stock price of a company, giving conservative investors more confidence in investing in the company. However, this does not always deliver value to shareholders (see below).
- Resource transfer: Resources are unevenly distributed across firms and the interaction of target and acquiring firm resources can create value through either overcoming information asymmetry or by combining scarce resources.
- Financial restructuring: A change in control can lead to a more cost-effective or safer capital structure, and more efficient use of financial assets.

- Business mix restructuring: The acquirer may divest noncore businesses.

The following motives are considered not to add shareholder value:

- Diversification: While this may hedge a company against a downturn in an individual industry it fails to deliver value, since it is possible for individual shareholders to achieve the same hedge by diversifying their portfolios at a much lower cost than those associated with a merger.
- Overextension: Tend to make the organization fuzzy and unmanageable.
- Manager's hubris: Manager's overconfidence about expected synergies from M&A which result in overpayment for the target company.
- Empire Building: Managers have larger companies to manage and hence more power.
- Manager's compensation: In the past, certain executive management teams had their payout based on the total amount of profit of the company, instead of the profit per share, which would give the team a perverse incentive to buy companies to increase the total profit while decreasing the profit per share (which hurts the owners of the company, the shareholders); although some empirical studies show that compensation is rather linked to profitability and not mere profits of the company.
- Bootstrapping: Example: how ITT executed its merger.
- Vertical integration: Companies acquire part of a supply chain and benefit from the resources.

1.4 Acquisitions and Growth

There are numerous reasons for a company to want to grow. Growth is often reckoned vital to the health of a company. A stagnating company may have difficulty attracting high-quality management. Furthermore, larger companies may pay higher salaries to top management than smaller companies. In some industries, size itself may bring competitive advantages. For example, marketing dominance may be strengthened through improved access to advertising. In addition, a large company may have significantly higher production or distribution efficiencies than a smaller one. Sometimes growth is a means of survival. For example, companies in the telecommunications industry have grown through acquisition in an effort to compete to control phone lines, cable systems, and content. The merger of Viacom, Blockbuster, and Paramount created a conglomeration of television and movie production, video distribution and publishing, and cable channels in an industry where many companies are merging to compete to become comprehensive media powerhouses. Firms in the defense industry have merged to survive in a declining market. Finally, tax laws may encourage merger growth. Despite these reasons to grow, growth by itself does not necessarily benefit either the stockholders or the managers of a company. Growth is not something that must be achieved regardless of its price. Throughout this course, emphasis will be placed on an acquisition's impact on value. Careful comparisons between benefits and costs will be made. A good acquisition will be defined as one that can be expected to increase the stock price (other things being equal) of the acquiring company. Furthermore, a merger is not always the best way to grow. A company can achieve internal expansion through investment in projects generated within the company itself. By doing so, efficiency may be improved, existing activities may be expanded, and new products may be introduced. External expansion takes place through an acquisition. Because of the similarities between the acquisition and the capital budgeting process, the same approval and review forms, control procedures, and post-audit examinations commonly used for analyzing capital expenditures can be applied to an acquisition analysis as well. In addition, consideration should be given at the highest levels of the business to how the proposed acquisition fits in with the needs and strategic thrust of the company. With a good fit, even at a relatively high price, the company being considered may be viewed as a good investment. Without a good fit, the acquisition may not be a good deal at almost any price.

1.5 Financial Analysis

An acquisition is essentially an investment decision. An initial outlay is invested to obtain expected future benefits. A good acquisition will generate greater benefits, in present value terms, than its costs. The likely effect of a good acquisition will be to increase the stock value of the acquiring company. To properly conduct this type of acquisition analysis, some strategic concepts and many valuation tools are required. The discipline of corporate finance shapes both the strategic and the financial analysis necessary to identify and evaluate acquisition candidates and assess the impact of acquisitions on company value. Acquisitions are financial decisions that should be consistent with the company's goal of shareholder wealth maximization. Sound and thorough financial analysis should be a part of any acquisition. Many acquisitions that fail, in the sense that they do not add value to the acquiring company, do so because they were motivated by wishful thinking rather than sound and thorough financial analysis. This discipline starts with the methods for analyzing a company's financial statements. The next step is an understanding of lenders' and investors' required returns and corporate valuation analysis. Through this framework, the financial analyst will be better able to view the acquisition process as a competition with other stock purchasers, all of whom are looking for good buys. Acquisitions are also strategic decisions that should be consistent with the mission of the acquiring company and fit into its overall strategic plan. The reasons for an acquisition must be understood in the context of a company's strategic analysis. Acquisitions can be justified in terms of the competitive advantages they produce (for example, marketing positions may be strengthened or production costs reduced). Other motives include improved management, tax benefits, or defensive maneuvers to prevent takeover by other companies. Finally, many acquisitions produce benefits purely from the financial and business restructuring that follows a change in control—as illustrated by the value increases following LBOs.

1.6 Accounting for Mergers

Two methods of accounting for acquisitions—purchase and pooling of interests—are often discussed. Financial statements that record the results of an acquisition must follow one of these two techniques. Financial managers must be aware of the accounting requirements as merger negotiations near completion. Under the purchase method, the acquired company is treated by the acquiring company as an investment, analogous to a capital budgeting expenditure. A totally new ownership is assumed. Asset values are reappraised in light of estimates of their current market values, and the balance sheet is restated to the new levels. As a result of these adjustments, goodwill often results. Goodwill is the amount by which the price paid for a company exceeds the company's estimated net worth at market value. Goodwill must be written off against future net income over a reasonable period. Such deductions against income are deductible for tax purposes in most countries. Under the pooling of interests' method, the assets and liabilities of the two combining companies are simply added together. Since only the book values of the assets and liabilities are considered, no goodwill results. In most countries, there are severe restrictions on a company's use of the pooling of interests' method. As a result of these restrictions, the pooling of interests' method is used much less today than it was in the past.

1.7 Merger Negotiation and Due Diligence

Negotiating the merger can be difficult. The simple answer to making it work is: hire the best advisors. Their job is to manage the negotiation process in such a way that it reaches a satisfactory conclusion—both parties must see a gain and both parties must be protected—and it does not run afoul of legal and regulatory constraints. The goal is to reach an agreement that is embodied in the "sale and purchase agreement"—which includes all the key terms of the deal, such as price, payment method, adjustments, constraints on the seller, etc., as well as accounting definitions, accounting and tax warranties, indemnities, etc. Quite often, a proposed merger or acquisition gets canned or valued down following conflicts over intellectual property rights, personnel, accounting discrepancies, or incompatibilities in integrating information technology systems. The process of researching, understanding and, in some cases, avoiding these risks is known as due diligence.

"Due diligence is going in and digging a hole in the ground and seeing if there's oil, instead of taking someone's word on it," says Joseph Bankoff, a lawyer. "If you don't do a sufficient amount of due diligence, you don't really know what questions to ask." Due diligence for mergers and acquisitions requires broad and deep data analysis of assets and liabilities, including large balance sheet items such as accounts receivable, inventory, and accounts payable to establish fair market value. It also means analyzing collections of receivables and inventory to identify doubtful accounts or obsolete stock, and analyzing cash receipts and billing files using historical trends to assess the reliability and adequacy of projected cash flows. The due diligence team must sift through press reports and regulatory filings to uncover any actual or potential legal, environmental, or other problems. In the case of a technology acquisition, a due diligence investigation should answer pertinent questions such as whether an application is too bulky to run on the mobile devices the marketing plan calls for or whether customers are right when they complain about a lack of scalability for a high-end system. Due diligence entails taking all the "reasonable steps" to ensure that both buyer and seller get what they expect "and not a lot of other things that you did not count on or expect," Bankoff explains. The process involves everything from reading the fine print in corporate legal and financial documents such as equity vesting plans and patents to interviewing customers, corporate officers, and key developers. It helps to identify potential risks and red flags.

1.8 Financing the Deal

Mergers are generally differentiated from acquisitions partly by the way in which they are financed and partly by the relative size of the companies. Various methods of financing an M&A deal exist: A company acquiring another will frequently pay for the other company with cash. Such transactions are usually termed acquisitions rather than mergers because the shareholders of the target company are removed from the picture and the target comes under the (indirect) control of the bidder's shareholders alone. An acquisition can involve a cash and debt combination, or a combination of cash and stock of the purchasing entity, or just stock. A "merger" or "merger of equals" is often financed by stocks deal (a stock swap), known in the UK as an all-share deal. Such deals are considered a merger rather than acquisitions because neither company pays money, and the shareholders of each company end up as the combined shareholders of the merged company. There are two methods of merging companies in this way:

- one company takes ownership of the other, issuing new shares in itself to the shareholders of the company being acquired as payment or
- a third company is created which takes ownership of both companies (or their assets) in exchange for shares in itself issued to the shareholders of the two merging companies.

Where one company is notably larger than the other, people may nevertheless be wary of calling the deal a merger, as the shareholders of the larger company will still dominate the merged company. Whenever cash is paid, the cash can be raised in a number of ways. The company may have sufficient cash available in its account, but this is unlikely. More often the cash is borrowed from a bank, or raised by an issue of bonds, or of equity. Acquisitions financed through debt are known as LBOs, and the debt will typically be moved down onto the balance sheet of the acquired company. Many leveraged acquisitions include a component of mezzanine debt, which falls between senior secured bank debt and equity.

1.9 Post-merger Integration

Some problems must inevitably occur when two companies combine; however, these problems can be anticipated and minimized. Managers of the acquired company will feel some loss of autonomy since their decisions must now be meshed with the policies of the merged company. Once-simple procedures become complicated by a new control system. Furthermore, the acquired company's managers are often concerned about personal recognition, advancement, and job security in the new company. Historically, many managers of acquired companies have lost their jobs following an acquisition.

Problems in the acquiring company will emerge as well. Its strengths and weaknesses and the skills and potential of its personnel will not be immediately apparent in the combined company. In addition, the staff of the acquiring company may lack the expertise to understand completely the production processes of the acquired company and may therefore be unable to make appropriate decisions about them. Disciplines, procedures, and controls that have been well established over time may not work as well in the new environment. There may be a clash of corporate cultures.

1.10 Cultural Issues in Cross-Border M&A

Corporate culture refers to the manner in which a company conducts its business. It begins with the general concept of how the senior management team wants to operate the business, and percolates down through the organization in the form of management structure, how decisions are made, policies and procedures, the types of people hired, and even its marketing efforts. When two firms from two different cultures merge, the success or failure of the newly created entity would depend, in part, on the fusion between the two corporate cultures. Management culture, leadership style, communication style, workplace environment, dress code, work hours' flexibility, special events for employees, and political activities are among the issues to be addressed. The Mercedes-Benz and Chrysler failure illustrates well the issue. In the late 1990s, the amalgamation of the two companies produced an industrial giant with global sales of more than $150 billion, making it fifth among the world's car manufacturers. Despite the strengths of each company taken alone, German and American mindsets and world views differ sharply. Mercedes-Benz was known for its excellence in engineering and product quality. Chrysler, on the other hand, reported an average profit per vehicle that was the highest among the then big-3 (GM, Ford, and Chrysler). Nonetheless, the challenge for the newly formed entity was to adequately integrate the two entities and achieve efficiencies that led to the merger. Five years later, differing behavioral habits and attitudes irritated both sides; this situation was exacerbated by the maintenance of the fiction that the amalgamation was a merger of equals. It was nothing of the sort.

> German and American commonalities such as work ethic, bluntness, lack of tact, a linear approach to tasks and time, punctuality, following agendas, results-orientation and emphasis on competitive prices and reliable delivery dates created a potential 'modus operandi', but two different mindsets led to irritation and misunderstanding on both sides. The German board member listed dozens of incidents.[8]

[8] Michael Gates (2016): Cross-Cultural Issues Relating to the DaimlerChrysler Merge—Case Study.

CHAPTER 2

Economic Effects of Antitrust Laws on Mergers and Acquisitions

2.1 General

By deterring anticompetitive practices, competition policy seeks to make markets work effectively and foster efficiency. That is, the aim of competition policy is to ensure that firms undertake the least possible number of behaviors that reduce social welfare by impairing competition.[1] Although most economists, from Adam Smith to its disciples, agree that competition works in the general interest, there is no such consensus on the ability of competition policy to be socially beneficial.[2] Effective competition policy ought to address both public and private restrictions on competition. The abuse of power by dominant market players or the price-fixing by a cartel is in the radar of competition agencies worldwide. Competition policy interventions rarely target productivity growth directly, instead they focus on promoting or preserving competition itself, often measured by lower prices or other consumer benefits.[3]

[1] Paolo Buccirossi and Lorenzo Ciari (2011): Competition Policy and Productivity Growth: An Empirical Assessment, Düsseldorf Institute for Competition Economics (DICE), p. 24.

[2] Paolo Buccirossi and Lorenzo Ciari (2011): Competition Policy and Productivity Growth: An Empirical Assessment, Düsseldorf Institute for Competition Economics (DICE), p. 12.

[3] OECD (2014): Factsheet on How Competition Policy Affects Macro-Economic Outcomes, p. 14.

F. I. Lessambo, *Mergers in the Global Markets*,
https://doi.org/10.1007/978-3-030-43558-5_2

2.2 Antitrust Law Objectives

To obtain the benefits that flow from competitive markets, governments need competition laws that deter anticompetitive conduct by dominant firms.[4] Effective competition laws aim to prevent:

- firms from colluding with their competitors to restrict competition either through price-fixing or market-sharing arrangements;
- firms with significant market power from abusing it to exclude competitors and to limit competition; and
- mergers between competitors that are not justified by efficiency gains that would outweigh any loss of competition.[5]

2.3 Competition Laws and Market Efficiency

2.3.1 Efficiency Assessment in the European Union

Under the EU Mergers Guidelines, in assessing whether a proposed concentration gives rise to a significant impediment to effective competition, efficiencies are an important factor of the assessment, on the basis of which intervention against a merger may ultimately not be warranted. However, the Commission has never cleared any proposed merger based on efficiencies that offset competitive harm. On the contrary, the Commission has in the recent past made antitrust prohibition decisions that have discarded the efficiency claims made by the parties.[6] The Commission is even open to consider all objective economic efficiencies in EU antitrust and merger proceedings, such as "static and dynamic" efficiencies, "allocative, productive and dynamic efficiencies" or "cost and qualitative" efficiencies.[7] All efficiency claims must be substantiated by the party asserting them in order to allow the Commission the time needed

[4] OECD (2012): Competition Policy: Promoting Efficiency and Sound Market, p. 9.

[5] OECD (2012): Competition Policy: Promoting Efficiency and Sound Market, p. 3.

[6] Cases COMP/34.579—MasterCard, COMP/36.518—Euro-Commerce and COMP/38.580—Commercial Cards, Decision C (2007)6474 final of 19 December 2007, upheld on appeal by the General Court on 24 May 2012 in Case T-111/08 MasterCard [2012] ECR II-not yet reported.

[7] OECD (2012): The Role of Efficiency Claims in Antitrust Proceedings, p. 90.

to assess or verify their nature natures; the causal link between the agreement and the alleged efficiencies; the likelihood and magnitude of each of the asserted efficiencies; and how and when each of the claimed efficiencies would be achieved.[8] Nonetheless, the asserted efficiencies need to be a direct consequence of the merger and cannot be achieved by less harmful alternatives. Moreover, they need to be foreseeable and substantial, and the benefit to in the form of price reductions or improvements of non-price parameters.[9] It should be noted that the Commission only takes into consideration those efficiencies that offset the harm suffered by the consumer groups that are adversely affected by the restrictive agreement, unilateral practice, or merger.

2.3.2 Competition and Market Efficiency in the United States

Efficiency is a broad economic term that may refer to allocative efficiency (allocation of resources to their most efficient use), productive efficiency (production in the least costly way), or dynamic efficiency (rate of introduction of new products or improvements of products and production techniques).[10]

In the United States, both the Federal Trade Commission and the Antitrust Division of the Department of Justice had recognized the consideration of efficiencies in the analysis of both mergers and non-merger conduct is an important aspect when evaluating whether a merger or conduct on balance harms competition.[11] For instance, merger efficiencies may increase the firm's ability to compete, and may benefit consumers through lower prices, improved quality, enhanced service, or new products.[12] However, the US Merger Guidelines state that efficiencies are most likely to make a difference in merger analysis when the likely adverse competitive effects, absent the efficiencies, are not great. Additionally,

[8] OECD (2012): The Role of Efficiency Claims in Antitrust Proceedings, p. 92.

[9] OECD (2012): The Role of Efficiency Claims in Antitrust Proceedings, p. 93.

[10] ICN (2011): Report on Competition Enforcement and Consumer Welfare.

[11] OECD (2012): The Role of Efficiency Claims in Antitrust Proceedings, p. 189.

[12] U.S. Department of Justice and Federal Trade Communication, Horizontal Merger Guidelines (hereinafter Merger Guidelines) § 10 (2010), available at http://www.justice.gov/atr/public/guidelines/hmg-2010.pdf.

efficiencies would almost never justify a merger to monopoly or near-monopoly.[13] The parties alleging efficiency bear the burden of the proof. Both the FTC and DOJ agencies never consider efficiency claims that are vague, speculative, or otherwise cannot be verified by reasonable means.

2.3.3 Competition and Market Efficiency in China

Under China AML, efficiency is achieved through equality of social distribution. Thus, the key purpose of the AML consists of eliminating monopoly in the markets, protecting the competition in the markets, and maintaining the market competition order, so that the markets can play a full role in allocating resources.[14] According to competition theory and industry economics, "effective monopoly" plays an important role in improving the development of economy. Therefore, the target of the anti-monopoly law should not aim at all monopoly enterprises but the monopoly and limit-competition behaviors.[15]

2.4 Competition Laws and Consumer Welfare

2.4.1 Competition Laws and Consumer Welfare in the EU

In assessing the effect of completion, "the European Commission generally applies an approach which endeavors to assess the effects an agreement, unilateral conduct or a concentration has on competition and consumer welfare. Such an approach entails the identification of the potential anti-competitive effects on parameters of competition such as price, quantity, product quality and variety, and innovation, as well as the pro-competitive effects, notably efficiencies."[16] The Court of Justice of the European Union has recently confirmed that dominant companies have the opportunity to advance efficiency arguments in order to justify conduct which may otherwise be regarded as abusive.[17]

[13] US Merger Guidelines § 10.

[14] Lin Shi (2009): Research on the Efficiency of China's Anti-Monopoly Law, *Asian Social Science*, p. 97.

[15] Idem.

[16] OECD (2012): The Role of Efficiency Claims in Antitrust Proceedings, p. 89.

[17] Case C-209/10 Post Denmark [2012] ECR I-not yet reported, paragraphs 41 et seq.

2.4.2 Competition Laws and Consumer Welfare in the United States

For the very first time, in United States v. Citizens & S, Nat'l Bank,[18] the US Supreme Court conceding to the authority of the Chicagoans and some Harvard Business School scholars switched from market efficiency to consumer welfare as the new standard. The facts of the case can be summarized as follows:

- Citizens and Southern Bank was the predominant bank in the Atlanta, Georgia area. Its Atlanta offices increased from three in 1946 to more than 100 by 1975. C&S and the next two largest banks in the Atlanta area control approximately 75 percent of the local banking business.
- For many years, Georgia prohibited banks located in cities from opening suburban branches. To circumvent Georgia's longstanding stringent restrictions on city banks' opening branches in suburban areas, Citizens & Southern National Bank (C&S National) formed a holding company, which then embarked on a program of forming de facto branch banks in Atlanta's suburbs.
- C&S filed the charter applications for the new branch banks, which in form were independent corporations. Each of the branch banks was a "correspondent associate" in the C&S system, with five percent of their stock owned by C&S's holding company.
- Each de facto branch was required to use its own judgment in setting rates and charges; as mandated by the antitrust laws in force.
- In 1970, Georgia amended its banking statutes to allow *de jure* branching upon a county-wide basis. This meant that C&S could now absorb the 5-percent banks as true branches because Atlanta is contained within the two counties encompassing the suburbs in which the 5-percent banks operated.
- Consequently C&S applied to the Federal Deposit Insurance Corporation (FDIC) under the Bank Merger Act of 1966 for permission to acquire all the stock of six of the 5-percent banks historically operated as de facto branches or "correspondent associate" banks within the C&S system.
- The FDIC authorized five of the proposed acquisitions.

[18] US SC 442 US 86, 131 n.1 (1975).

- The Government then brought suit in District Court for injunctive relief, alleging that the five acquisitions would lessen competition in relevant banking markets in violation of § 7 of the Clayton Act, and that the historic de facto branch relations between C&S and the six 5-percent banks constituted unreasonable restraints of trade in violation of § 1 of the Sherman Act.
- Put differently, the Government argued that the correspondent associate relationship went far beyond the normal correspondent bank relationship and therefore unreasonably restrained competition among the five percent banks and between those banks and C&S.
- The court rendered judgment for C&S. Three of the 5-percent banks were formed prior to, and three after, July 1, 1966. The "grandfather" provision of the Bank Holding Company Act, 12 U.S.C. § 1849(d), as added by the 1966 amendments, provides that

  "Any acquisition, merger, or consolidation of the kind described in [12 U.S.C. §] 1842(a)… which was consummated at any time prior or subsequent to May 9, 1956, and as to which no litigation was initiated by the Attorney General prior to July 1, 1966, shall be conclusively presumed not to have been in violation of any antitrust laws other than."
- The SC held that:

  "Since the Attorney General took no action by July 1966, against the three 5-percent banks that were formed prior to that date, the transactions by which these banks became 5-percent banks fall within the terms of the grandfather provision of the Bank Holding Company Act, and therefore the correspondent associate programs in force at these banks are immune from attack under § 1 of the Sherman Act."

While C&S's formation of a de facto branch was a unique type of transaction, it may fairly be characterized as an "acquisition, merger, or consolidation of the kind described in [12 U.S.C. §] 1842(a)," and clearly falls within the class of dealings by bank holding companies that Congress intended, in the grandfather provision, to shield from retroactive challenge under the antitrust laws.

Further, the Court held that it was therefore pro-competitive for C&S to circumvent the law by providing new banking options while not eliminating existing ones. The US Supreme Court's decision in C&S constituted a departure from traditional notions concerning the per se illegality of price-fixing. As Professor Velvel[19] put it: "In holding that an anticompetitive restraint such as price fixing can be justified if it stems from a procompetitive relationship, the Court broke away from the reluctance of recent years to permit such restraints."

2.4.3 *Competition Laws and Consumer Welfare in China*

As other competition laws around the world, the AML is designed to promote the welfare of Chinese consumers by shielding them from the potential negative effects of monopolistic conduct, especially the creation of market power and the resulting price increases. Article 1 of the AML states: "This law will be enacted for the purpose of guarding or ceasing monopolistic conduct, safeguarding and promoting the order of market competition, improving economic efficiency, protecting the consumer's interest, protecting the public interest, and promoting the healthy development of the socialist market economy." Likewise, Article 7 of the AML, which deals with state-owned enterprises, states: "With respect to the industries controlled by state-owned economy and concerning the lifeline of national economy and national security...the State shall protect the lawful business operations...and shall supervise and control the business operations of and the prices of commodities and services... to protect the consumer interests and facilitate technological progress."

2.5 The Economic Effects of Competition on Mergers and Acquisitions

In general, competition laws operate as a shield to protect and safeguard against the possibility that firms may acquire market power through mergers and acquisitions. However, the objectives of antitrust laws have evolved through the times. Stemming from market efficiency to economic growth to social welfare.

The fundamental problem in this area is that the Supreme Court has, over the past 40 years, dramatically narrowed the reach of the Sherman

[19] Lawrence R. Velve (1976): Carving Holes in the Sherman Act: A Comment on the Citizens & Southern Case, *Catholic University Law Review*, Vol. 25, p. 543.

Act.[20] The court loosening interpretation of the market efficiency standard embedded in the Sherman Act led to significant growth of "superstar firms" growth and concentration at the expense of their smaller, less efficient rivals, causing various measures of broad industry concentration in the US economy.

2.5.1 Decline in Enforcement

In 2017, 2052 proposed transactions were reported to the antitrust authorities, of which 51 received an in-depth investigation and 21 were subject to an enforcement action.[21] This statistics, alone, seems to indicate a substantial decline in the review. The treatment of proposed mergers under US antitrust law has become much more lenient without Congress changing the substantive standard to be used for merger review and without any updated guidance from the Supreme Court, which has not heard a merger case since 1974.[22] The swift in the standard stemmed mainly from the work produced by the publications from the Chicago School of Business, Harvard Business School, and others. Chicago School figures have helped inspire the courts to raise the standards that plaintiffs must satisfy to prevail with predatory pricing claims.[23] Lower Courts, in the absence of clear guidance from the US Supreme Court, embraced the standard change without providing a clear rationale. For instance, in 1990, the DC Circuit, departed from the precedent established by the Supreme Court in the 1960s, which stated:

> Evidence of market concentration simply provides a convenient starting point for a broader inquiry into future competitiveness.[24]

[20] Carl Shapiro (2019): Protecting Competition in the American Economy: Merger Control, Tech Titans, Labor Markets, *Journal of Economic Perspectives*, Vol. 33, No. 3, Summer 2019, p. 70.

[21] Federal Trade Commission and Department of Justice 2018.

[22] Carl Shapiro (2019): Protecting Competition in the American Economy: Merger Control, Tech Titans, Labor Markets, *Journal of Economic Perspectives*, Vol. 33, No. 3, Summer 2019, p. 74.

[23] William E. Kovacic (2007): The Intellectual DNA of Modern U.S. Competition Law for Dominant Firm Conduct: The Chicago/Harvard Double Helix, *Columbia Business Law Review*, Vol. 1, pp. 6–7.

[24] United States vs. Baker Hughes, 908 F.2d 981, at 984.

The US antitrust agencies buy into the arguments developed by the elite economists reducing both the threshold of presumption and making antitrust challenges inaccessible to the average plaintiff. Both the Department of Justice and the Federal Trade Commission put more weight on direct evidence of competitive effects and less weight on market shares.[25] To interpret an observed increase/decrease in market concentration, a trap to avoid consist of avoiding the data from the US economic census. Rising concentration resulting from increased efficiency by one or a few firms reflects the competitive process at work; rising concentration caused by mergers may well reflect a decline in competition.

2.5.2 *The Reasons for the Decline*

The reason for the decline is twofold. *First*, the agencies enforcements (FTC and the Antitrust Division of the DOJ) have reduced their missions to look solely on mergers in highly concentrated markets, and rely on self-evidence safe harbor to justify or approve all other mergers viewed as unlikely to have adverse competitive effects and ordinarily require no further analysis.[26] A safe harbor was set up. The enforcement agencies become unlikely to challenge a horizontal merger if the post-merger concentration of the market would be less than 1000 on the Herfindahl Index.[27] The HHI of 1000 was raised to 1500 in the 2010 Merger Guidelines. Those guidelines stated that "mergers resulting in un-concentrated markets are unlikely to have adverse competitive effects and ordinarily require no further analysis." However, the 2010 Mergers Guidelines provided no empirical justification for this statement or for the increase in the HHI threshold. Further, empirical studies of the HH1000 threshold reveal that significant number of mergers satisfying the safe harbor conditions result in price increases. For instance, Kwako study looking at nine mergers where the post-merger HHI is less than 1500, found that seven mergers resulted in

[25] Carl Shapiro (2019): Protecting Competition in the American Economy: Merger Control, Tech Titans, Labor Markets, *Journal of Economic Perspectives*, Vol. 33, No. 3, Summer 2019, p. 74.

[26] John Kwoka (2017): The Structural Presumption and the Safe Harbor in Merger Review: False Positives or Unwarranted Concerns? *Antitrust Law Journal*, Vol. 81, p. 841.

[27] William F. Smith (1982): Changing Enforcement Policy, *Antitrust Law Journal*, Vol. 51, No. 95, p. 101.

price increases.[28] *Second*, the judicial branch, and specifically the US Supreme Court reliance on such economic research in articulating its presumption concerning the role of market structure in merger analysis. Numbers alone are telling: since 1999, the DOJ has brought only one major monopolization case under Section 2 of the Sherman Act. In contrast, the DOJ, between 1970 and 1972, brought 39 civil and 3 criminal cases against monopolies and oligopolies. The DOJ brought its last predation case in 1999.[29] As this trend continues, some observers have argued that the shift is more likely to be harmful to consumer welfare interest whom the enforcement agencies purport to protect.

2.5.3 The Pursuit of an Uncertain Goal

Competition officials during the last Bush administration stated that the "promotion of consumer welfare and the organization of the free market economy are the only goals of its antitrust laws…with other economic or social objectives better pursued by other instruments."[30] However, there is no consensus as to the meaning of the pursued goal at the center of the antitrust enforcement. A Report on the Objectives of Unilateral Conduct Laws, Assessment of Dominance/Substantial Market Power, and State-Created Monopolies by the International Competition Network,[31] found that thirty of the thirty-three respondents that addressed the questions on objectives state that their unilateral conduct rules aim to promote consumer welfare. However, most respondents do not specifically define consumer welfare and appear to have different economic understandings of the term. Thus, some agencies focus on short-term consumer surplus, while others apply a longer-term welfare concept that also accounts for productivity and innovation (for example, the Netherlands response states that "competition law should not solely concentrate on short-term

[28] John Kwoka (2017): The Structural Presumption and the Safe Harbor in Merger Review: False Positives or Unwarranted Concerns? *Antitrust Law Journal*, Vol. 81, p. 864.

[29] Marshall Steinbaum and Maurice E. Stuke (2018): The Effective Competition Standards, The Roosevelt Institute, pp. 8–9.

[30] Marshall Steinbaum and Maurice E. Stuke (2018): The Effective Competition Standards, The Roosevelt Institute, p. 11.

[31] The 6th Annual Conference of the ICN Moscow, May 2007.

price/output issues but should also [maintain] a dynamic perspective taking due account of innovation)."[32]

2.5.4 *The Unfitness of the Welfare Protection Standard*

In Reiter v. Sonotone Corp.,[33] the US Supreme Court, quoting Robert Bork, declared that "Congress designed the Sherman Act as a 'consumer welfare prescription.'" Prior to that mainland ruling, antitrust inquiries have always focused on competitive effects, or at least this has been their perceived intent.[34] In so doing, the Supreme court departed from the Court's long-established understanding of the goal of antitrust laws.[35] Though the Sherman Act was passed without any specific debate over the merit of competition, the contemporaneous debate leads to the crux of the act, which was to prevent competition. For instance, before the Senate voted on the Judiciary Committee's bill, Senator Hoar stated:

> The great thing that this bill does, except affording remedy, is to extend the common-law principles, which protected fair competition in trade in old times in England, to international and interstate commerce.[36]

Indeed, prior to the Reitner case, the notion that competition was the goal of US competition laws appeared to be uncontroversial. For instance, the 1955 report of the Attorney General's National Committee to Study the Antitrust Laws opened with a simple statement:

> The general objective of the antitrust laws is promotion of competition in open markets.[37]

[32] Idem, p. 8.

[33] Reiter v. Sonotone Corp., 442 U.S. 330, 343 (1979).

[34] Barak Orbach (2013): How Antitrust Lost Its Goal, *Fordham Law Review*, Vol. 81, No. 5, p. 2254.

[35] Idem, p. 2261.

[36] Idem, p. 2262.

[37] Report of the Attorney General's National Committee to Study the Antitrust Laws 1 (1955).

Almost, all lower courts acknowledged competition was the goal of US competition laws.[38] Even a year before its reversal, the US Supreme Court, in National Society of Professional Engineers v. United States (NSPE),[39] the high court recognized that competition was the crux of the antitrust legislation. Justice Stevens stated that "Under antitrust law, competition analysis is narrow and does not include welfare effects."[40]

Robert Bork thesis, which has introduced the nebulous concept of consumer welfare as a substitute to competition has acquired its "title of nobles" and had acquired political significance in the United States. It is worthy to mention that in the mid-1970s, when the phrase "consumer welfare" was gaining popularity, Robert Bork served as the US Solicitor General.[41] The harm to consumers is often less adjudicated or investigated. In general, when courts and commentators refer to consumer welfare, often they really mean the welfare of trading partners.[42]

2.6 The Harmfulness of Some Currently Approved M&A

A merger can be harmful to consumers when the purchasing firm uses that merger as a means to restrict competition and consumer choice. That is often the case in industries where there is already limited competition (i.e., the airline industry or the cable industry). Some mergers have created challenges for new entrants (i.e., aspiring entrepreneurs and innovators) to join a given industry. The megamergers that have taken place over the past 30 years in pharmaceuticals, among/between big airlines, or big banks have not improved customers' welfare. Instead, some megamergers like AT&T and Time Warner have crushed customer welfare. Microsoft bought LinkedIn, Amazon merged with Whole Foods and Monsanto merged with Bayer. In 2011 alone, Google bought all its minor

[38] City of Lafayette v. La. Power & Light Co., 435 U.S. 389, 398 (1978); Brown Shoe Co. v. United States, 370 U.S. 294, 330 (1962); Standard Oil Co. v. FTC, 340 U.S. 231, 248–49 (1951).

[39] Nat'l Soc. of Prof'l Eng'rs v. United States, 435 U.S. 679 (1978).

[40] Idem, Id. 695–96.

[41] Barak Orbach (2013): How Antitrust Lost Its Goal, *Fordham Law Review*, Vol. 81, No. 5, p. 2273.

[42] C. Scott Hemphill and Nancy L. Rose (2018): Mergers That Harm Sellers, *The Yale Law Journal*, p. 2091.

competitors, almost every week. Facebook has acquired both Instagram and WhatsApp[43] at the expense of innovation, creativity, and economic growth. Tech and communications firms today are like the railroads of old.[44]

As Professor John Colley put it:

> Generally speaking, as industries consolidate down to fewer players, prices increase because there is less competition....You tend to end up with less choice of products too.[45]

2.7 Raise of Concentration

Concentration has been steadily rising and competition declining in a great many sectors of the economy.[46] Council of Economic Advisors provides evidence that firms' profits are now concentrated in the very top firm or firms in each industry more than ever before—and those firms have an ever higher probability that their profits will persist over time.[47] For instance, in the high-tech industry, successive mergers[48] have extended the reach of the tech company's dominance. They make entry into their core business more difficult by suppressing outside firms that might pose an eventual threat to that core business. In so doing, the top firms have consolidated their market power and prevent the emergence of future

[43] Zephyr Teachout (2018): Megamergers Like AT&T and Time Warner Crush American Democracy, *The Guardian*.

[44] Rana Foroohar (31 July 2014): Why Big Mergers Are Bad for Consumers, TIME.COM.

[45] By Daniel Thomas (30 October 2015): Are Big Mergers Bad for Consumers? Business Reporter.

[46] Three rating agencies control 95 percent of the market for rating bonds and other financial instruments: Moody's, Standard & Poor's, and Fitch. Four airlines control 80 percent of domestic airline seat capacity. The four largest food companies control 82 percent of beef packing, 85 percent of soybean processing, 63 percent of pork packing, and 53 percent of chicken processing. Nearly 90 percent of all internet searches now go through Google.

[47] John E. Kwoka, Jr. (2019): "Does America Have a Monopoly Problem? Examining Concentration and Competition in the US Economy", Testimony Before United States Senate Committee on the Judiciary Subcommittee on Antitrust, Competition Policy, and Consumer Rights, p. 3.

[48] Microsoft's acquisition of LinkedIn or Skype, and Facebook's acquisitions of Instagram and WhatsApp.

competition.[49] That so as the enforcement agencies have narrowed their threshold looking solely on mergers in highly concentrated markets at the expense of others. Consequently, this policy shift has in fact permitted numerous mergers that have harmed competition and consumers.[50] To reverse, the concentration trend, some authors, have argued that the enforcement agencies should take advantage of the structural presumption set up by the US Supreme Court in U.S. v. Philadelphia National Bank,[51] laying the burden of proof to the merger's parties. That is, the shift in the burden of proof to the prospective merging companies to demonstrate that "to-be-acquired firm" is not capable of being a serious competitor in the near future.[52] Also, the enforcement agencies would need to expand the scope of horizontal mergers to include "potential competition" whenever needed.[53] Some may argue that the doctrine of "potential competition" would not move the needle as the US Supreme Court has already set up a higher threshold of proof for the agencies to overcome a merger eliminating a potential competitor.[54] As explained earlier, the judicial has replaced the ultimate goal of M&A review from protection competition to ensuring the consumer welfare.

[49] John E. Kwoka, Jr. (2019): "Does America Have a Monopoly Problem? Examining Concentration and Competition in the US Economy", Testimony Before United States Senate Committee on the Judiciary Subcommittee on Antitrust, Competition Policy, and Consumer Rights, p. 5.

[50] Idem, p. 6.

[51] U.S. v. Philadelphia National Bank, 374 U.S. 321 (1963).

[52] John E. Kwoka, Jr. (2019): "Does America Have a Monopoly Problem? Examining Concentration and Competition in the US Economy", Testimony Before United States Senate Committee on the Judiciary Subcommittee on Antitrust, Competition Policy, and Consumer Rights, p. 12.

[53] John E. Kwoka, Jr. (2019): "Does America Have a Monopoly Problem? Examining Concentration and Competition in the US Economy", Testimony before United States Senate Committee on the judiciary Subcommittee on Antitrust, Competition policy, and Consumer Rights, p. 8.

[54] U.S. v. Marine Bancorporation, 418 U.S. 602 (1974). It required (a) that the outside firm have the requisite "characteristics, capabilities, and economic incentives," (b) that the firm be unique or at least one of very few such well-positioned firms, and (c) that there was actual evidence that such a firm had "in fact tempered oligopolistic behavior" by incumbents. The first two of these criteria are unexceptional, but the third proof of actual past effect is quite different than for mergers between incumbents, and far harder to establish.

PART II

The Competition and National Security Reviews

CHAPTER 3

M&A Policies Review Under the Competition and National Security Laws in the United States

3.1 General

The core US antitrust law that applied for mergers reviews are (i) the Sherman Antitrust Act in 1890, (ii) the Clayton Act of 1914, (iii) the Hart–Scott–Rodino Antitrust Improvements Act ("HSR"), (iv) the Federal Trade Commission Act, and (v) the Foreign Trade Antitrust Improvements Act. The enforcement of the antitrust laws is managed by two distinct federal agencies: The Department of Justice (antitrust division) and the federal trade commission. Antitrust laws protect consumers from anticompetitive conduct such as a firm's acquisition of the ability to raise prices above levels that would prevail in a competitive market. Both horizontal and vertical mergers fall within the ambit of these provisions. The antitrust laws were enacted for the protection of competitions not competitors. Put differently, the US federal antitrust law was enacted to combat powerful trusts and monopolies arising from the post-Civil War industrialization.[1]

3.1.1 *The Sherman Act of 1890*

Enacted in 1890, the Sherman Antitrust Act was the first measure enacted by the US Congress to prohibit trusts. It was based on the constitutional

[1] Ariel Ezrachi (2015): Sponge, University of Oxford Centre for Competition Law and Policy, Working Paper CCLP (L) 42, p. 8.

F. I. Lessambo, *Mergers in the Global Markets*,
https://doi.org/10.1007/978-3-030-43558-5_3

power of Congress to regulate interstate commerce. The Sherman Act was generated by a sense of angry frustration with Standard Oil and the large new enterprises that seemed to be increasingly dominating more ordinary Americans' lives.[2]

Section 1 of the Act provides:

> Every contract, combination in the form of trust or otherwise, or conspiracy, in restraint of trade or commerce among the several States, or with foreign nations, is declared to be illegal.

However, Section 6a of the Act provides, under specific conditions, an exemption with respect to foreign nations. Conduct involving trade or commerce with foreign nations:

> Sections 1 to 7 of this title shall not apply to conduct involving trade or commerce (other than import trade or import commerce) with foreign nations unless:
>
> (1) such conduct has a direct, substantial, and reasonably foreseeable effect (a) on trade or commerce which is not trade or commerce with foreign nations, or on import trade or import commerce with foreign nations; or (b) on export trade or export commerce with foreign nations, of a person engaged in such trade or commerce in the United States; and
>
> (2) such effect gives rise to a claim under the provisions of sections 1 to 7 of this title, other than this section.

In the late 1990s, in another effort to ensure a competitive free market system, the Federal Government used the Sherman Act, then over 100 years old, against Microsoft—the giant computer software company.

Penalties for violating the act can range from civil to criminal penalties; an individual violating these laws may be jailed for up to three years and fined up to $350,000 per violation. Corporations may be fined up to $10 million per violation.

3.1.2 *The Clayton Act of 1914*

- Section 4 of the Clayton Act is essentially a remedial provision, and provides treble damages to any person who shall be injured in his business or

[2] Donald I. Baker and John DeQ. Briggs (2004): Rethinking U.S. Antitrust Policy and Administration: Joining the Rest of the World in the 21st Century, p. 4.

property by reason of anything forbidden in the antitrust laws. Section 4 of the Clayton Act provide in full:

"[A]ny person who shall be injured in his business or property by reason of anything forbidden in the antitrust laws may sue therefore in any district court of the United States in the district in which the defendant resides or is found or has an agent, without respect to the amount in controversy, and shall recover threefold the damages by him sustained, and the cost of suit, including a reasonable attorney's fee."

For plaintiffs in an antitrust action to recover treble damages on account of § 7 violations, they must prove more than that they suffered injury which was causally linked to an illegal presence in the market; they must prove injury of the type that the antitrust laws were intended to prevent and flows from that which makes the defendants' acts unlawful. The injury must reflect the anticompetitive effect of either the violation or of anticompetitive acts made possible by the violation.

- Section 7 of the Clayton Act prohibits acquisitions, including mergers, where in any line of commerce or in any activity affecting commerce in any section of the country, the effect of such acquisition may be substantially to lessen competition, or to tend to create a monopoly.

3.1.3 The Cellar–Kefauver Act of 1950

The Cellar–Kefauver Act of 1950, extended Section 7 of the Clayton Act to cover mergers as well as stock acquisitions of competitors.

3.1.4 The Scott–Hard–Rodino Improvement Act of 1982

In 1976, under the Hart–Scott–Rodino Antitrust Improvement, the United States moved to require premerger notification for mergers reaching certain fixed revenue thresholds. Under the Hart–Scott–Rodino Act, the FTC and the Department of Justice review most of the proposed transactions that affect commerce in the United States and are over a certain size, and either agency can take legal action to block deals that it believes would "substantially lessen competition." Although there are some exemptions, for the most part current law requires companies to report any deal that is valued at more than $78.2 million to the agencies so they can be reviewed.

3.1.5 *The Federal Trade Commission Act*

Section 13(b) provides for the grant of a preliminary injunction where such action would be in the public interest as determined by a weighing of the equities and a consideration of the Commission's likelihood of success on the merits. However, the FTC is not required to establish that the proposed merger would in fact violate Section 7 of the Clayton Act.

Whenever the Commission has reason to believe that a corporation is violating, or is about to violate, Section 7 of the Clayton Act, the FTC may seek a preliminary injunction to prevent a merger pending the Commission's administrative adjudication of the merger's legality.

To establish its prima facie first instance jurisdiction, the FTC must establish (i) likelihood of success on the merits and (ii) the principal public equity weighing in favor of the issuance of preliminary injunctive relief. The whole point of a preliminary injunction is to avoid the need for intrusive relief later, since even with the considerable flexibility of equitable relief, the difficulty of "unscrambling merged assets" often precludes an effective order of divestiture.

- The likelihood of success on the merits

To determine the likelihood of success on the merits the courts measure the probability that, after an administrative hearing on the merits, the Commission will succeed in proving that the effect of the merger may be substantially to lessen competition, or to tend to create a monopoly in violation of Section 7 of the Clayton Act. The standard for the likelihood of success on the merits is met if the FTC has raised questions going to the merits so serious, substantial, difficult and doubtful as to make them fair ground for thorough investigation, study, deliberation and determination by the FTC in the first instance and ultimately by the Court of Appeals. To rebut the presumption, the defendants must produce evidence that "show[s] that the market-share statistics [give] an inaccurate account of the [merger's] probable effects on competition" in the relevant market. Market concentration, or the lack thereof, is often measured by the Herfindahl–Hirschmann Index (HHI). Further, the anticompetitive effect of the merger is further enhanced by high barriers to market entry. Once the FTC has established the prima facie case, the defendant still can rebut the presumption of Section 7 (Clayton Act). If the defendant successfully rebuts the presumption (of illegality), the burden of producing additional evidence of anticompetitive effect shifts to the government, and merges with the ultimate burden of persuasion, which remains with the government at all times. To succeed in the rebuttal, the defendant must argue (i) the extent of the premerger competition, (ii) the post-merger efficiencies, (iii) the merger is necessary for innovation, and (iv) the structural market barriers to collusion.

- The weighing of public equities

The principal public equity weighing in favor of the issuance of preliminary injunctive relief is the public interest in effective enforcement of the antitrust laws.

3.1.6 The Foreign Trade Antitrust Improvements Act

The FTAIA amended the Sherman Act to expressly limit those circumstances in which the Act applies to foreign conduct. The Foreign Trade Antitrust Improvements Act amended both the Sherman Act and the federal Trade Commission Act. It amended Section 6 of the Sherman Acts to be read as follows:

> § 6a. Conduct involving trade or commerce with foreign nations
> Sections 1 to 7 of this title [i.e., the Sherman Act] shall not apply to conduct involving trade or commerce (other than import trade or import commerce) with foreign nations unless
>
> (1) such conduct has a direct, substantial, and reasonably foreseeable effect
> (A) on trade or commerce which is not trade or commerce with foreign nations, or on import trade or import commerce with foreign nations; or
> (B) on export trade or export commerce with foreign nations, of a person engaged in such trade or commerce in the United States; and
>
> (2) such effect gives rise to a claim under the provisions of Sections 1 to 7 of the Sherman Act, other than this section. If Sections 1 to 7 of this title apply to such conduct only because of the operation of paragraph (1)(B), then Sections 1 to 7 of this title shall apply to such conduct only for injury to export business in the United States.

To limit the extraterritorial application of US antitrust law, Sections 6a(1)(A) and (2) provide that the Sherman Act shall not apply to conduct involving trade or commerce (other than import trade or import commerce) with foreign nations, unless such conduct has a direct, substantial, and reasonably foreseeable effect on trade or commerce which is not trade or commerce with foreign nations, or on import trade or import commerce with foreign nations, and also, in either case, unless the "effect on import trade or domestic commerce gives rise to a claim under federal antitrust law." Put differently, there must be a direct, substantial, and reasonable foreseeable effect on US domestic commerce; and the effect must give rise to a federal antitrust claim.

The Supreme Court has warned that rampant extraterritorial application of US laws creates a serious risk of interference with a foreign nation's ability independently to regulate its own commercial affairs.

3.1.7 The Department of Justice (DOJ) Antitrust Enforcement Unit

The antitrust laws in the United States have both a criminal and civil nature. They allow aggrieved parties to file for either a felony crime or to seek for financial damages. In criminal cases, the DOJ acts as a prosecutor. Since May 1999, more than 40 foreign defendants have served, or are serving, prison sentences in the United States for participating in an international cartel or for obstructing an investigation of an international cartel. Foreign nationals from France, Germany, Japan, the Republic of Korea, Norway, the Netherlands, Sweden, Switzerland, Chinese Taipei, and the United Kingdom are among those defendants.[3]

The DOJ cartel enforcement tools include:

(i) Rogatory request letter: Letters rogatory are formal requests for judicial assistance made by a court in one country to a court in another country. They are meant to obtain evidence that may not be accessible to a foreign criminal or civil litigant without judicial authorization. Compliance with a letter rogatory request is left to the discretion of the court or tribunal in the requested jurisdiction.

[3] OECD (2014): Challenges of International Co-operation in Competition Law Enforcement, p. 35.

(ii) Sealed indictment: A secret indictment made by the grand jury, formally charging the accused of a crime, is kept sealed until the accused has been arrested, notified of the charges, or released from jail pending trial.

- The Marine Hose Conspiracy case:

Marine hose is a flexible rubber hose used to transfer oil between tankers and storage facilities and/or buoys. The parties (coconspirators) agreed to rig bids, fix prices, and allocate market shares for marine hose.

Five companies (Parker, Bridgestone Corp. of Japan, Manuli Spa of Italy's Florida subsidiary, Trelleborg of France, and Dunlop Marine and Oil Ltd. of the United Kingdom) and eight individuals have pleaded guilty.

- Pisciotti was initially arrested in Germany on June 17, 2013.
- In April 2014, Germany extradited Romano Pisciotti, an Italian national, to the United States to face criminal charges related to his alleged participation in an international cartel in the marine hose industry. Mr. Pisciotti's extradition represented the first time that the Antitrust Division of the US Department of Justice ("DOJ") had obtained the extradition of a foreign national solely based on antitrust charges.
- Pisciotti was extradited under the terms of the US–Germany extradition treaty, which, like most extradition treaties, provides for a "dual criminality" requirement.
- Pisciotti entered a guilty plea with the US DOJ Antitrust Division.
- On April 24, 2014, the district court in the Southern District of Florida sentenced Romano Pisciotti to two years in prison after he pleaded guilty to a one-count felony indictment for participating in a conspiracy to rig bids, fix prices, and allocate market shares of marine hose sold in the United States and abroad.

(ii) Interpol Red Notices: Red Notices are one of the ways in which INTERPOL (the International Criminal Police organization) informs its member countries that an arrest warrant has been issued for an individual by a judicial authority and seeks the location and arrest of wanted persons with a view to extradition or similar lawful action. It is important for prosecutors to make certain that the case is significant enough to warrant placing their offices under such a burden in deciding whether or not to request the issuance of a Red Notice.

3.2 FTC–DOJ Procedure

Since the Hart–Scott–Rodino Act, M&A are under prenotification regime. That is, the parties planning an acquisition or a transaction of a certain size[4] are required to notify both the DOJ and the FTC of their planned transaction. The parties need to submit minimal information about their revenues, shareholders, and shareholdings, as well as certain transaction-related documents that address competition, markets, entry, and other antitrust-relevant points. The parties may, depending on the case, make presentations to the agency regarding potential antitrust concerns, as well as their advisors' (economists) arguments as to why the transaction does not raise antitrust issues. The provided information is kept confidential by both agencies. The agencies have thirty business days from the date they receive all relevant data to review the proposed transaction under the competitive antitrust laws. The agencies may seek additional information and extend the waiting period until thirty days after obtaining that information from the parties. If the agencies found that there is no antitrust violation, the parties can go ahead and close their deal. On the reverse, if the agencies found that the proposed deal presents significant potential to the antitrust laws, they have to convince a federal court that the proposed transaction would violate Section 7. If the agency challenges the transaction, the parties may consider offering remedies (i.e., asset or business divestitures), or conduct restriction agreements, to address the agency's antitrust concerns. Very often the agencies come up with a settlement proposal with the parties that allow the transaction to go with specific amendments. If, extraordinarily, no agreement is reached, the FTC or DOJ will have to seek a preliminary injunction from a District Judge. The FTC staff can also seek a preliminary injunction from a federal court enjoining the parties from closing while they proceed under administrative procedure before an Administrative Law Judge and eventual review by the full Commission itself.

[4] The current threshold is about $60 million.

Once the agencies have established to the satisfaction of the District Judge that a structural presumption of concentration does exist, the parties can still rebut such a presumption by bringing forth the evidence of either the ease of entry or the efficiencies within the challenged market. It should be noted that the Antitrust analyses begins with the study of the market power as provided by the FTC–DOJ Guidelines for Horizontal Mergers.[5] The Guidelines proceed in five steps to examine the market competition:

- Market: Concentration and share

When the agencies identify a potential competitive concern with a horizontal merger, market definition plays two roles: (i) market definition helps specify the line of commerce and section of the country in which the competitive concern arises and (ii) market definition allows the agencies to identify market participants and measure market shares and market concentration. The Guidelines retain the basic hypothetical monopolist test used since 1982 to define relevant markets. The agencies employ the hypothetical monopolist test to evaluate whether groups of products in candidate markets are sufficiently broad to constitute relevant antitrust markets. The hypothetical monopolist test requires that a product market contain enough substitute products so that it could be subject to post-merger exercise of market power significantly exceeding that existing absent the merger.

> The Agencies use the hypothetical monopolist test to identify a set of products that are reasonably interchangeable with a product sold by one of the merging firms.

When applying the hypothetical monopolist test to define a market around a product offered by one of the merging firms, if the market includes a second product, the agencies will normally also include a third product if that third product is a closer substitute for the first product than the second product. The measurement of market shares and market concentration is not an end in itself, but is useful to the extent it illuminates the merger's likely competitive effects.

[5] www.ftc.gov›tips-advice›guide-antitrust-laws.

Market concentration and market share data are normally based on historical evidence. Market concentration is often one useful indicator of likely competitive effects of a merger. In evaluating market concentration, the agencies consider both the post-merger level of market concentration and the change in concentration resulting from a merger. The agencies give more weight to market concentration when market shares have been stable over time, especially in the face of historical changes in relative prices or costs. The agencies may measure market concentration using the number of significant competitors in the market. This measure is most useful when there is a gap in market share between significant competitors and smaller rivals or when it is difficult to measure revenues in the relevant market.

The agencies often calculate the Herfindahl–Hirschman Index ("HHI") of market concentration (Fig. 3.1). The HHI is calculated by summing the squares of the individual firms' market shares, and thus gives proportionately greater weight to the larger market shares. When using the HHI, the agencies consider both the post-merger level of the HHI and the increase in the HHI resulting from the merger. The increase in the HHI is equal to twice the product of the market shares of the merging firms. However, the HHI thresholds will not be applied as rigid screens and that other competitive factors will be examined to determine whether increased concentration at any level will lead to adverse competitive effects. Based on their experience, the agencies generally classify markets into three types:

THE HHI

- The **Herfindalhl–Hirschman Index (HHI)** is a measure of concentration within an industry and is often used by regulators to evaluate the effects of a merger.
- The HHI is constructed as the sum of the squared market shares of the firms in the industry:

$$\text{HHI} = \sum_{i}^{n}\left(\frac{\text{Output of firm } i}{\text{Total sales or output of the market}} \times 100\right)^2$$

HHI Concentration Level and Possible Government Action			
Post-Merger HHI	Concentration	Change in HHI	Government Action
Less than 1,000	Not concentrated	Any amount	No action
Between 1,000 and 1,800	Moderately concentrated	100 or more	Possible challenge
More than 1,800	Highly concentrated	50 or more	Challenge

Fig. 3.1 The Herfindahl–Hirschman Index (*Source* Adapted from FTC and DOJ, https://www.justice.gov›atr›herfindahl-hirschman-index)

- Unconcentrated Markets: HHI below 1500
- Moderately Concentrated Markets: HHI between 1500 and 2500
- Highly Concentrated Markets: HHI above 2500

Example 3.1. Consider the nonalcoholic beverage industry has six core companies

Companies	*Market share (%)*
Algeria	25
Bulgaria	15
Comoria	15
Danubia	15
Erudia	15
Ferunia	15
	100

Task: What is the likely government action, if the companies Erudia and Ferunia combined?

Solution

Companies	*Market share (%)*	*HHI before*	*Companies*	*Market share (%)*	*HHI after*
Algeria	25	625	Algeria	25	625
Bulgaria	15	225	Bulgaria	15	225
Comoria	15	225	Comoria	15	225
Danubia	15	225	Danubia	15	225
Erudia	15	225	Erudia + Ferunia	30	900
Ferunia	15	225			
Total	100	1125		100	1575

The industry would be considered moderately concentrated before and after the concentration of Erudia and Ferunia.

The change in the HHI is (1575-1125) 450, may trigger government agencies' challenges.

The agencies then use the market shares to assess market concentration before and after the proposed acquisition. Market shares may not fully reflect the competitive significance of firms in the market or the impact of a merger. They are used in conjunction with other evidence of competitive effects. That is, the agencies may conclude that a merger raises competitive concerns without identifying a precise relevant market if there is evidence that the merger is likely to result in anticompetitive effects.

- Adverse competitive effects

The 2010 Guidelines specify two types of potential competitive effects: (i) unilateral effects and (ii) coordinated interaction.

(i) Unilateral effects

Unilateral effects address whether the merged firm will have an incentive to raise prices on its own even if competitors do not also raise their prices in response. The agencies consider whether the merger will allow the merged firm unilaterally to raise prices or reduce output in a way that harms customers. There are a variety of methods to assess the unilateral effects of a proposed merger.[6]

(ii) Coordinated effects

Coordinated effects address whether the merger will increase the likelihood that firms in the relevant market will jointly raise prices. The agencies also consider whether the merger will increase opportunities for coordinated interaction. Coordinated interaction involves conduct by multiple firms that is profitable for each of them only as a result of the accommodating reactions of the others. These reactions can blunt a firm's incentive to offer customers better deals by undercutting the extent to which such a move would win business away from rivals. They also can enhance a firm's incentive to raise prices, by assuaging the fear that such a move would lose customers to rivals. The ability of rival firms to engage in coordinated conduct depends on the strength and predictability of

[6] Estimating a diversion ratio; Conducting merger simulations; and Using the Gross Upward Pricing Pressure Index.

rivals' responses to a price change or other competitive initiative. A market typically is more vulnerable to coordinated conduct if a firm's prospective competitive reward from attracting customers away from its rivals will be significantly diminished by likely responses of those rivals.

- Powerful buyers

The agencies consider the possibility that powerful buyers may constrain the ability of the merging parties to raise prices. However, the agencies do not presume that the presence of powerful buyers alone forestalls adverse competitive effects flowing from the merger. Even buyers that can negotiate favorable terms may be harmed by an increase in market power. The agencies examine the choices available to powerful buyers and how those choices likely would change due to the merger. Normally, a merger that eliminates a supplier whose presence contributed significantly to a buyer's negotiating leverage will harm that buyer.

- Entry analysis

The prospect of entry into the relevant market will alleviate concerns about adverse competitive effects only if such entry will deter or counteract any competitive effects of concern so the merger will not substantially harm customers. A merger is not likely to enhance market power if entry into the market is so easy that the merged firm and its remaining rivals in the market, either unilaterally or collectively, could not profitably raise the price or otherwise reduce competition compared to the level that would prevail in the absence of the merger.

- Efficiencies

Competition usually spurs firms to achieve efficiencies internally. Efficiencies also may lead to new or improved products, even if they do not immediately and directly affect the price. However, efficiencies are difficult to verify and quantify, in part because much of the information relating to efficiencies is uniquely in the possession of the merging firms.

Therefore, it is incumbent upon the merging firms to substantiate efficiency claims so that the agencies can verify by reasonable means the likelihood and magnitude of each asserted efficiency, how and when each would be achieved (and any costs of doing so), how each would enhance the merged firm's ability and incentive to compete, and why each would be merger-specific. The agencies will not challenge a merger if cognizable efficiencies are of a character and magnitude such that the merger is not likely to be anticompetitive in any relevant market. Other efficiencies, such as those relating to research and development, are potentially substantial but are generally less susceptible to verification and may be the result of anticompetitive output reductions.

- Failing firm defense

The agencies do not normally credit claims that the assets of the failing firm would exit the relevant market unless all of the following circumstances are met: (1) the allegedly failing firm would be unable to meet its financial obligations in the near future; (2) it would not be able to reorganize successfully under Chapter 11 of the Bankruptcy Act; and (3) it has made unsuccessful good-faith efforts to elicit reasonable alternative offers that would keep its tangible and intangible assets in the relevant market and pose a less severe danger to competition than does the proposed merger.

- Partial acquisitions

The agencies also review acquisitions of minority positions involving competing firms, even if such minority positions do not necessarily or completely eliminate competition between the parties to the transaction. Partial acquisitions that do not result in effective control may nevertheless present significant competitive concerns and may require a somewhat distinct analysis from that applied to full mergers or to acquisitions involving effective control.

3.3 Remedies

Courts are clothed with large discretion to create remedies effective to redress (antitrust) violations and to restore competition. Indeed, divestiture is a common form of relief from unlawful mergers. Further, an antitrust violator "may... be required to do more than return the market to the status quo ante. Courts may not only order divestiture but may also order relief" designed to give the divested (firm) an opportunity to establish its competitive position. Further, the courts have the power to grant relief on the FTC's complaint, despite the mergers having taken place, and that instance, the case would not be considered moot.

3.4 M&A Review Under National Security Laws in the United States

Several tests organized the review process under the national security reviews of foreign investments in the United States.

3.4.1 The National Defense Act of 1950 (as Amended)[7]

Section 721 of the Defense Production Act (as amended) grants The Secretary of Chairperson of the Committee on Foreign Investment the authority to review certain mergers, acquisitions, and takeovers that may have an impact on the US national security interests. The term "national security" is construed so as to include those issues relating to "homeland security," including its application to critical infrastructure. The authority of the Committee to initiate a review may not be delegated to any person, other than the Deputy Secretary or an appropriate Under Secretary of the department or agency represented on the Committee. The Committee immediately conducts an investigation of the effects of a covered transaction on the national security of the United States, and takes any necessary actions in connection with the transaction to protect the national security of the United States.

Further, Section 721a of the Defense Production Act states:

No entity controlled by a foreign government may merge with, acquire, or take over a company engaged in interstate commerce in the

[7] 50 U.S.C. App. § 2170.

United States that: (1) is performing a Department of Defense contract, or a Department of Energy contract under a national security program, that cannot be performed satisfactorily unless that company is given access to information in a proscribed category of information or (2) during the previous fiscal year, was awarded Department of Defense prime contracts in an aggregate amount in excess of $500,000,000; or Department of Energy prime contracts under national security programs in an aggregate amount in excess of $500,000,000.

3.4.2 *The Committee on Foreign Investment in the United States*

Established in 1975, the Committee on Foreign Investment in the United States was mandated to review the acquisition of US firms by foreign entities that could compromise US national security. The CFIUS operates pursuant to Section 721 of the Defense Production Act of 1950, as amended by the Foreign Investment and National Security Act (FINSA) and as implemented by Executive order 11858.

3.4.3 *The Exon–Florio Amendment to the Defense Production Act*

In 1988, Congress decided to strengthen the CFIUS review process by passing the Exon–Florio amendment. The Exon–Florio amendment to the Defense Production Act authorizes the President to suspend or prohibit transactions that could result in foreign control of US companies if the transaction threatens to impair national security. The Exon–Florio provision grants the President broad discretionary authority to take what action he considers to be "appropriate" to suspend or prohibit proposed or pending foreign acquisitions, mergers, or takeovers which "threaten to impair the national security."

3.4.4 *The Homeland Security Act of 2002*

In this act, Congress provided for special support for "critical infrastructure," which it defined as:

> systems and assets, whether physical or virtual, so vital to the United States that the incapacity or destruction of such systems and assets would have a debilitating impact on security, national economic security, national public health or safety, or any combination of those matters.

3.4.5 The Foreign Investment and National Security Act of 2007

In July 2007, the Foreign Investment and National Security Act of 2007 amended Exon–Florio to, among other things, expand the factors to be considered in deciding what could affect national security and bring greater transparency to the CFIUS review process. The FINSA definition of critical infrastructure used by CFIUS does not exactly match the USA PATRIOT Act definition of critical infrastructure used by the Department of Homeland Security. FINSA defines the term as, "systems and assets," whether physical or virtual, so vital to the United States that the incapacity or destruction of such systems or assets would have a debilitating impact on national security. The list of factors for CFIUS members to consider before approving a deal grew from five to twelve. The amended list includes the following:

(1) Domestic production needed for projected national defense requirements;
(2) The capability and capacity of domestic industries to meet national defense requirements, including the availability of human resources, products, technology, materials, and other supplies and services;
(3) The control of domestic industries and commercial activity by foreign citizens as it affects the capability and capacity of the United States to meet the requirements of national security;
(4) The potential effects of the transactions on the sales of military goods, equipment, or technology to a country that supports terrorism or proliferates missile technology or chemical and biological weapons; and transactions identified by the Secretary of Defense as "posing a regional military threat" to the interests of the United States;
(5) The potential effects of the transaction on US technological leadership in areas affecting US national security;
(6) Whether the transaction has a security-related impact on critical infrastructure in the United States;
(7) The potential effects on US critical infrastructure, including major energy assets;
(8) The potential effects on US critical technologies;
(9) Whether the transaction is a foreign government-controlled transaction;

(10) In those cases involving a government-controlled transaction, a review of (A) the adherence of the foreign country to nonproliferation control regimes, (B) the foreign country's record on cooperating in counterterrorism efforts, and (C) the potential for transshipment or diversion of technologies with military applications;
(11) The long-term projection of the US requirements for sources of energy and other critical resources and materials; and
(12) Such other factors as the President or the Committee determine to be appropriate.

Congress states that the purpose of the Act is to ensure national security while promoting foreign investment and the creation and maintenance of jobs and to reform the process by which such investments are examined for any effect they may have on national security.

3.4.6 The Foreign Investment Risk Review Modernization Act of 2018 (FIRRMA)

FIRRMA provides a comprehensive revision of the CFIUS process, and allows the President of the United States to block or suspend proposed or pending foreign mergers, acquisitions, or takeovers by or with any foreign person that could result in foreign control of any US business, including such a merger, acquisition, or takeover carried out through a joint venture that threatens to impair the national security (Fig. 3.2). However, to invoking such authority the President must conclude that (i) other US laws are inadequate or inappropriate to protect the national security and (ii) he/she must have "credible evidence" that the foreign interest exercising control might take action that threatens to impair the national security.[8] Moreover, FIRRMA shifts the filing process for foreign firms from voluntary to mandatory in certain cases and provides for a two-track method for reviewing investment transactions, with some transactions requiring a declaration to CFIUS and receiving an expedited process, while transactions involving investors from countries of special concern would require a written notification of a proposed transaction and would

[8] CRS (2019): The Committee on Foreign Investment in the United States (CFIUS) Updated August 6, 2019, p. 10.

CFIUS Legislative History

1975 CFIUS established by Executive Order.

1988 "Exon-Florio" amendment to Defense Production Act. Codified the process CFIUS used to review foreign investment transactions.

1992 "Byrd Amendment" to Defense Production Act. Required reviews in cases where foreign acquirer was acting on or in behalf of a foreign government.

2007 Foreign Investment and National Security Act of 2007 replaced Executive Order and codified CFIUS.

2018 Foreign Investment Risk Review Modernization Act of 2018 provided a comprehensive reform of the CFIUS process.

Fig. 3.2 CFIUS legislative history (*Source* Congressional Research Service, 2019. Original source can be accessed at https://crsreports.congress.gov/product/pdf/RL/RL33388)

receive greater scrutiny.[9] Furthermore, FIRRMA Modifies CFIUS' annual reporting requirements, including its annual classified report to specified Members of Congress and nonclassified reports to the public to provide for more information on foreign investment transactions.[10]

The purpose of the national security reviews conducted by CFIUS is to allow CFIUS to identify and address any national security risk that arises as a result of a covered transaction, and, in the circumstances described in § 800.506(b) of the regulations, to request that the President determine whether to suspend or prohibit a covered transaction or take other action. National security considerations are facts and circumstances, with respect to a transaction, that have potential national security implications and that

[9] CRS (2019): The Committee on Foreign Investment in the United States (CFIUS) Updated August 6, 2019, p. 11.

[10] CRS (2019): The Committee on Foreign Investment in the United States (CFIUS) Updated August 6, 2019, p. 11.

therefore are relevant for CFIUS to analyze in determining whether a transaction threatens to impair US national security.

The fact that a transaction presents national security considerations does not mean that CFIUS will necessarily determine that the transaction poses national security risk. The national security considerations presented by transactions that CFIUS has reviewed pertain to one or both of the following: (1) The nature of the US business over which foreign control is being acquired and (2) the nature of the foreign person that acquires control over a US business. Risk requires not only threat, but also vulnerability in US national security.

CFIUS does not issue advisory opinions as to whether a covered transaction raises national security considerations. Rather, it conducts full reviews of specific covered transactions that are notified to CFIUS pursuant to § 800.401 of the regulations. This guidance may provide assistance to parties as they consider whether to file a voluntary notice with CFIUS.

Only the President has the authority to suspend or prohibit a covered transaction. Pursuant to Section 6(c) of Executive Order 11858, CFIUS refers a covered transaction to the President if CFIUS or any member of CFIUS recommends suspension or prohibition of the transaction, or if CFIUS otherwise seeks a presidential determination on the transaction. In order to exercise the authority to suspend or prohibit a covered transaction under Section 721, the President is required to make two findings: (1) That there is credible evidence that leads the President to believe that the foreign interest exercising control might take action that threatens to impair the national security and (2) that provisions of law, other than Section 721 and the International Emergency Economic Powers Act ("IEEPA"), do not, in the judgment of the President, provide adequate and appropriate authority for the President to protect the national security. The President's decision is not subject to judicial review.

3.5 CFIUS Composition and Mandates

Originally established by an Executive Order of President Ford in 1975, the committee has operated until recently in relative obscurity. CFIUS is an interagency committee chaired by the Department of the Treasury and comprised of eight other voting members (the Departments of Commerce, Defense, Homeland Security, Justice, State, and Energy; the US Trade Representative; and the White House Office of Science and Technology); two permanent nonvoting members (the Director of National Intelligence and the Department of Labor); and several other White House offices that act as observers and, on a case-by-case basis, participate in CFIUS reviews.

3.6 CFIUS Review and Investigation

CFIUS is an interagency committee chaired by the Secretary of the Treasury that consists of members representing major executive departments and agencies. Thus, the formal part of the CFIUS review process ranges from 30 to 90 days. Most cases are concluded in the first 30 days and result in the transaction being approved without condition. CFIUS reviews, findings, and deliberations are confidential. Thus, it is not always easy for the parties involved and their lawyers to predict the outcome as the CFIUS and the President of the United States may consider a variety of factors in reaching out to their conclusions.

The CFIUS process helps to ensure the necessary balance between the protection of vital national security interests and the promotion of global investment in the US. The process formally begins when parties to a proposed or pending transaction jointly file a voluntary notice with all requested information under the CFIUS regulations.

CFIUS applies a three-part national security analysis to each transaction that it reviews: (i) it assesses whether the acquirer has the ability or intent to exploit or cause harm (the "threat analysis"); (ii) it considers the US business at issue, including its relationship to any weakness or shortcoming in the US national defense or any susceptibility to impairment of US national security (the "vulnerability analysis"); and (iii) it evaluates the consequences if threat and vulnerability interact as the result of a particular transaction (the "risk analysis") (Fig. 3.3).

The CFIUS process consists of several phases:

- First, there is a prefiling stage during which the parties to a transaction prepare the notice and preliminary consultations with committee staff may occur. Such early engagement of CFIUS staff is advisable, including the submission of a draft filing. If the file is deemed complete, then begins officially the review process.
- The second phase—a 30-day review period—begins once parties submit the notice and CFIUS deems it complete and disseminates

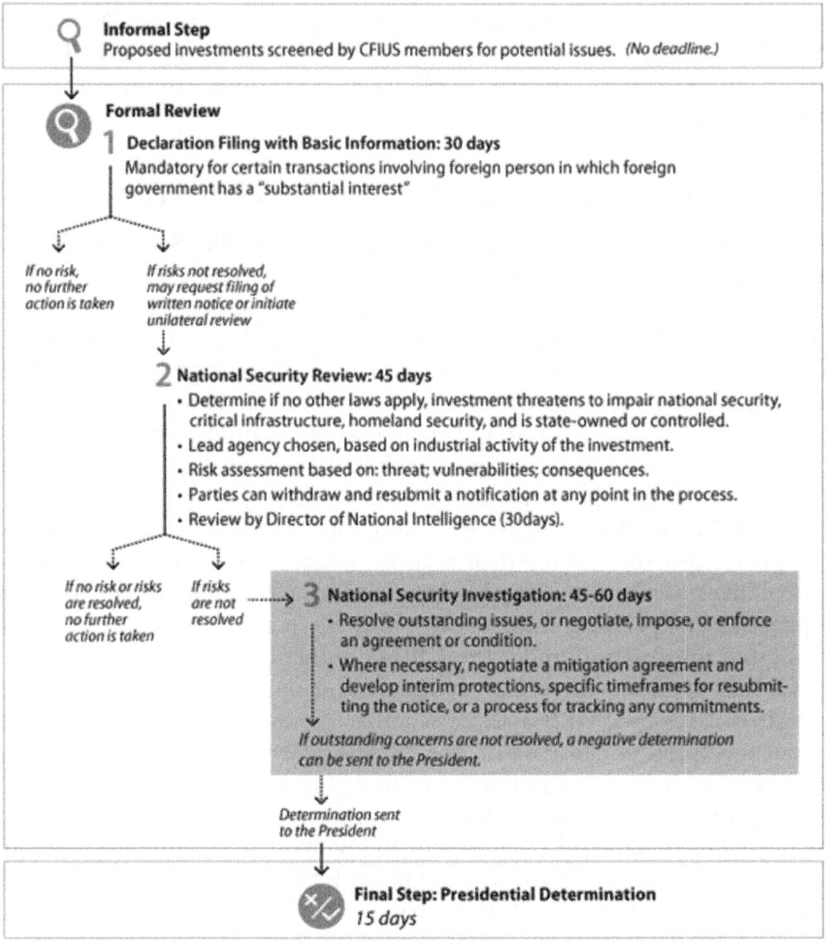

Fig. 3.3 CFIUS review process (*Source* Congressional Research Service, 2019. Original source can be accessed at https://crsreports.congress.gov/product/pdf/RL/RL33388)

it to CFIUS members. The Committee will not accept a notice until it has received the notice in both electronic and hard-copy forms. All files submitted electronically must be no larger than five megabytes (5 MB) in size to facilitate handling by the Committee. Larger files must be broken down into multiple files of 5 MB or less. Upon accepting a notice, the Staff Chairperson will advise the parties in writing of the date the review process begins and the date it will end.

During this phase, the committee reviews the transaction to determine the effects of the transaction on national security, using various factors set forth in the CFIUS regulations to make that determination. The Department of Treasury as Committee Chair may request additional information from the parties, who must respond within three business days, unless an extension is demanded and obtained.

- The third phase consists of an additional 45-day investigation of the effects of a covered transaction on national security. CFIUS must conduct this additional investigation if, during the initial review period, (i) it determines that the transaction (a) is a foreign government-controlled transaction, (b) would result in foreign control of any critical infrastructure of or within the United States and could impair national security, and such impairment was not mitigated during the initial review period, or (c) threatens to impair national security and the threat was not mitigated during the initial review period or (ii) the lead agency recommends, and CFIUS agrees, that an investigation should be undertaken.
- The fourth phase consists of giving clearance or referring the deal to the President.

The President of the United States has almost unlimited authority to take "such action for such time as the President considers appropriate to suspend or prohibit any covered transaction that threatens to impair the national security of the United States."[11]

Once the CFIUS has completed all action with respect to a covered transaction or the President of the US announced the decision not to exercise his authority under Section 721 with respect to the covered transaction, then the parties receive a "safe harbor" with respect to the transaction. However, if the CFIUS finds that a covered transaction presents national security risks and that other provisions of law do not provide adequate authority to address the risks, the CFIUS may enter into an agreement with, or impose conditions on, the parties to mitigate such risks, or

[11] 50 U.S.C. § 4565.

Covered Transaction by Sector and Year, 2009-2013					
Year	Manufacturing	Finance, Information, and Services	Mining, Utilities, and Construction	Wholesale, Retail, and Transportation	Total
2009	21 (32%)	22 (34%)	19 (29%)	3 (5%)	65
2010	36 (39%)	35 (38%)	13 (14%)	9 (10%)	93
2011	49 (44%)	38 (34%)	16 (14%)	8 (7%)	111
2012	45 (39%)	38 (33%)	23 (20%)	8 (7%)	114
2013	35 (36%)	32 (33%)	20 (21%)	10 (10%)	97
Total	**186 (39%)**	**165 (34%)**	**91 (19%)**	**38 (8%)**	**480**

Fig. 3.4 CFIUS covered transactions (*Source* Adapted from CFIUS, 2015. https://www.treasury.gov/resource-center/international/foreign-investment/Documents/Annual%20Report%20to%20Congress%20for%20CY2014.pdf)

it may refer the case to the US President for final determination. I come to wonder whether the CFIUS can reverse its approval decision if facts unknown to it at the time of the approval raise a serious issue of national security interest. The situation has never occurred in the United States in Germany in the Aixtron case where the German Ministry of industry withdrew it prior certificate of non-objection by reversing its course of action (Fig. 3.4).

3.7 Appealing the CFIUS Review Process

The CFIUS can and has been challenged under the "due process clause" of the US constitution, which requires that at least, the affected parties be informed of the actions undertaken, and be given access to the "evidence" upon which the final conclusion has been made.

- The Ralls case

  - Ralls Corp. an affiliate of the Chinese construction and machinery conglomerate Sany Group, purchased four American companies that were developing wind farms in Oregon.

- Ralls Corp. is a US company owned by two Chinese nationals, one of whom was also CFO of Sany Group, a Chinese manufacturing company, and the other the vice president of Sany Electric Company, Ltd.
- Ralls Corp. develops wind energy projects for wind turbines manufactured by its Sany affiliate.
- In March 2012, Ralls acquired four wind farm projects in Oregon near restricted military airspace maintained by the US Navy—without first seeking CFIUS review.
- The project sites overlap with a restricted airspace and bombing zone used by military aircraft out of Naval Air Station Whidbey Island.
- In June 2012, Ralls was informed that the US Department of Defense intended to invoke CFIUS review of the already-closed transactions.
- After review, CFIUS determined that the acquisition posed a national security threat, and ordered Ralls essentially to halt all activity at the wind farms and remove all items from the sites. Ralls was then also prohibited from selling the wind farms without first notifying CFIUS, which could object to any sale. With these restrictions in effect, CFIUS submitted its report to the White House, which subsequently ordered Ralls to divest itself of the US business, based on "credible evidence... that Ralls... might take action that threatens to impair the national security of the United States."
- Ralls Corp. challenged both the determinations of the CFIUS and the President's divesture Order under (i) the Administrative Procedure Act (APA) and (ii) both orders were unconstitutional under due process clause of the US constitution.[12] Put differently, Ralls alleged that neither the CFIUS nor the White House gave it notice of the evidence on which they relied in making their security determinations nor opportunity to rebut that evidence.
- In September 2012, the federal district court dismissed the case, finding that Ralls had no property interest subject to due process, since Ralls knew its acquisition was subject to CFIUS and presidential approval but nonetheless waived the opportunity to obtain a determination from CFIUS and the President by not submitting the transaction for review prior to closing.

[12] Both the Fifth and Fourteenth Amendments of the US Constitution.

- The District Court also determined that the fact that Ralls was given the ability to submit written arguments, met with CFIUS officials in-person, and answered follow-up questions was sufficient due process in light of the government's interest in protecting the national security of the United States.[13]
- On appeal, the DC Circuit held that Ralls' vested property interest could not be deprived without first notifying Ralls of the official action, providing Ralls access to the unclassified evidence on which the President relied, and affording Ralls an opportunity to rebut that evidence. Further, the Court found that other non-US-owned wind farms operate near the same restricted airspace.[14]
- The DC Circuit found that while Congress may have precluded judicial review of the final actions of the President "to suspend or prohibit any covered transaction that threatens to impair the national security of the United States," it does not preclude "the reviewability of a constitutional claim challenging the process preceding such presidential action."
- The Court of Appeal remanded the case to the DC District Court "with instructions that Ralls be provided… access to the unclassified evidence on which the President relied and an opportunity to respond thereto."
- On November 6, 2014, the DC District Court issued an order in accordance with the appellate court's decision,[15] requiring the executive to provide Ralls Corp. "with access to all unclassified material contained in the record compiled by CFIUS and all unclassified factual findings or evidence underlying CFIUS's recommendation to the President."[16]

[13] Ralls Corp. v. Comm. on Foreign Inv., 758 F.3d 296, 301 (D.C. Cir. 2014).

[14] Ralls Corp. v. Comm on Foreign Inv. in the United States, No. 13-5315 (D.C. Cir. July 15, 2014).

[15] Ralls Corp. v. Comm. on Foreign Inv., Nos. 12-1513, 12-2026 (ABJ), 2014 U.S. Dist. LEXIS 177868 (D.D.C. 2014).

[16] United Court of Appeals for the District of Columbia Circuit, No. 13-5316 (July 15, 2019).

3.8 CFIUS Case Study

3.8.1 Mamco Manufacturing

- In February 1990, President George H.W. Bush voided the sale of Mamco Manufacturing, a Seattle-based aircraft parts maker, to a Chinese state-owned aviation company.
- President George H.W. Bush ordered the state-owned China National Aerospace Technology Import and Export Corp. to divest its acquired interests in the Mamco Manufacturing, Inc.

3.8.2 CNOOC and Unocal

Prior to the signing of the Foreign Investment and National Security Act (FINRA) into law, the US Congress intervened to prevent Chinese oil giant China National Offshore Oil Company (CNOOC) from acquiring the California-based energy company Unocal.[17]

The relevant facts of the case are as follow:

- In June 2005, China National Offshore Oil Company (CNOOC) endeavored to acquire Unocal, a US petroleum company at $67 per share.
- CNOOC rival Chevron joined the bid in Unocal and offered Unocal $60 per share.
- CNOOC bid triggered a widespread public and US Congressional opposition. Congressional leaders from across the spectrum began to oppose the deal and urge President Bush to block it.
- On June 30, 2005, the House of Representatives voted 398 to 15 in favor of a nonbinding resolution that condemned the takeover as a threat to national security.
- On August 1, 2005, Unocal's board of directors recommended that shareholders take the Chevron offer because the CNOOC bid price did not sufficiently compensate Unocal shareholders for the higher risk of the CNOOC transaction.

[17] Destiny D. Dea (2008): The Costs of Perceived Hypocrisy: The Impact of US Treatment of Foreign Acquisitions of Domestic Enterprises, *Duke Law Review*, Vol. 57, No. 1795, p. 1801.

- On August 2, 2005, CNOOC withdrew its takeover offer for Unocal.
- The SEC subsequently approved Chevron's acquisition of Unocal for lesser than CNOOC bid.

It is worthy to note that the CFIUS did not reject the CNOOC bid, rather it was congressional opposition and the threat of overriding the teeth-less CFIUS, prior to the FINRA.

> The White House
> Office of the Press Secretary
> For Immediate Release
> September 28, 2012
> Order Signed by the President regarding the Acquisition of Four US Wind Farm Project Companies by Ralls Corporation
> ORDER
> \- - - - - - -
> By the authority vested in me as President by the Constitution and the laws of the United States, including Section 721 of the Defense Production Act of 1950, as amended (Section 721), 50 U.S.C. App. 2170,
> Section 1. Findings. I hereby make the following findings:
> (a) There is credible evidence that leads me to believe that Ralls Corporation (Ralls), a corporation organized under the laws of Delaware, and its subsidiaries, and the Sany Group (which includes Sany Electric and Sany Heavy Industries), a Chinese company affiliated with Ralls (together, the Companies); and, Mr. Dawei Duan (Mr. Duan) and Mr. Jialing Wu (Mr. Wu), citizens of the People's Republic of China and senior executives of the Sany Group, who together own Ralls; through exercising control of Lower Ridge Windfarm, LLC, High Plateau Windfarm, LLC, Mule Hollow Windfarm, LLC, and Pine City Windfarm, LLC (collectively, the Project Companies), all limited liability companies organized under the laws of Oregon, might take action that threatens to impair the national security of the United States and
> (b) Provisions of law, other than Section 721 and the International Emergency Economic Powers Act (50 U.S.C. 1701 et seq.), do not, in my judgment, provide adequate and appropriate authority for me to protect the national security in this matter.

Sec. 2. Actions Ordered and Authorized. On the basis of the findings set forth in Section 1 of this order, considering the factors described in Subsection 721(f), as appropriate, and pursuant to my authority under applicable law, including Section 721, I hereby order that:
(a) The transaction resulting in the acquisition of the Project Companies and their assets by the Companies or Mr. Wu or Mr. Duan is hereby prohibited, and ownership by the Companies or Mr. Wu or Mr. Duan of any interest in the Project Companies and their assets, whether directly or indirectly through owners, subsidiaries, or affiliates, is prohibited.
(b) In order to effectuate this order, Ralls shall divest all interests in:
(i) the Project Companies;
(ii) the Project Companies' assets, intellectual property, technology, personnel, and customer contracts; and
(iii) any operations developed, held, or controlled, whether directly or indirectly, by the Project Companies at the time of, or since, their acquisition
not later than 90 days after the date of this order, unless such date is extended for a period not to exceed three (3) months, on such written conditions as the Committee on Foreign Investment in the United States (CFIUS) may require. Immediately upon divestment, Ralls shall certify in writing to CFIUS that such divestment has been effected in accordance with this order.
(c) No later than 14 calendar days from the date of this order, the Companies shall:
(i) remove from the properties on which the Companies have proposed to construct wind farms (including alternate sites) that are identified in the notice filed with CFIUS (Properties) all items, structures, or other physical objects or installations of any kind (including concrete foundations) that the Companies or persons on behalf of the Companies have stockpiled, stored, deposited, installed, or affixed thereon and
(ii) provide CFIUS with a statement signed by Mr. Duan and Mr. Wu certifying that the Companies have completed such removal.
(d) The Companies, and any persons acting for or on behalf of the Companies, including officers, employees, and owners, shall cease all access, and will not have any access, to the Properties. Notwithstanding the foregoing, individuals that are US citizens contracted by the Companies and approved by CFIUS may access the Properties solely

for purposes of fulfilling the requirements of subsection (c) of this section.
(e) The Companies, Mr. Duan, and Mr. Wu shall not sell or otherwise transfer, or propose to sell or otherwise transfer, or otherwise facilitate the sale or transfer of, any items made or otherwise produced by the Sany Group to any third party for use or installation at the Properties.
(f) Ralls shall not complete a sale or transfer of the Project Companies or their assets to any third party until:
(i) all items, structures, or other physical objects or installations of any kind (including concrete foundations) that the Companies or persons on behalf of the Companies have stockpiled, stored, deposited, installed, or affixed on the Properties have been removed from the Properties and the Department of Defense has notified the Companies that it has verified the Companies' certification of such removal provided pursuant to subsection (c) of this section;
(ii) Ralls notifies CFIUS in writing of the intended recipient or buyer; and
(iii) Ralls has not received a provisional or final objection from CFIUS to the intended recipient or buyer within 10 business days of the notification in subsection f(ii) of this section. Among the factors CFIUS may consider in reviewing the proposed sale or transfer are whether the buyer or transferee: is a US citizen or is owned by US citizens; has or has had a direct or indirect contractual, financial, familial, employment, or other close and continuous relationship with the Companies or Project Companies, or their officers, employees, or owners; and can demonstrate a willingness and ability to support compliance with this order.
(g) From the date of this order until Ralls provides a certification of divestment to CFIUS pursuant to subsection (b) of this section, the Companies shall certify to CFIUS on a monthly basis that they are in compliance with this order.
(h) Without limitation on the exercise of authority by any agency under other provisions of law, and until such time as the divestment is completed and verified to the satisfaction of CFIUS, CFIUS is authorized to implement measures it deems necessary and appropriate to verify that operations of the Project Companies are carried out in such a manner as to ensure protection of the national security interests of the United States. Such measures may include but are not limited to the following: on reasonable notice to the Project

Companies and the Companies, employees of the US Government, as designated by CFIUS, shall be permitted access, for purposes of verifying compliance with this order, to all premises and facilities of the Project Companies and the Companies located in the United States:
(i) to inspect and copy any books, ledgers, accounts, correspondence, memoranda, and other records and documents in the possession or under the control of the Companies or the Project Companies that concern any matter relating to this order;
(ii) to inspect any equipment and technical data (including software) in the possession or under the control of the Companies or the Project Companies; and
(iii) to interview officers, employees, or agents of the Companies or the Project Companies concerning any matter relating to this order.
CFIUS shall conclude its verification procedures within 90 days after the divestment is completed.
(i) The Attorney General is authorized to take any steps necessary to enforce this order.
Sec. 3. Revocation of Prior Orders. CFIUS's Order Establishing Interim Mitigation Measures of July 25, 2012, and Amended Order Establishing Interim Mitigation Measures of August 2, 2012, are hereby revoked.
Sec. 4. Reservation. I hereby reserve my authority to issue further orders with respect to the Companies or the Project Companies as shall in my judgment be necessary to protect the national security.
Sec. 5. Publication and Transmittal.
(a) This order shall be published in the Federal Register.
(b) I hereby direct the Secretary of the Treasury to transmit a copy of this order to the appropriate parties named in Section 1 of this order.
BARACK OBAMA

3.8.3 The German–US Aixtron Case

- On December 2, 2016, President Obama issued an Executive Order blocking the proposed acquisition of Aixtron, Inc., a California-based US subsidiary of Aixtron SE ("Aixtron"), a German semiconductor firm, based upon the recommendation of the CFIUS.
- Aixtron, a publicly traded company organized and headquartered in Germany, manufactures equipment for the global semiconductor

industry, including systems used to build compound semiconductor materials.

- Aixtron's US business includes its wholly owned subsidiary, Aixtron, Inc., which is organized and headquartered in California.
- Aixtron's US subsidiary employs approximately 100 people at a facility in California.
- In the fiscal year 2015 alone, the United States accounted for more than one-fifth of Aixtron's sales. Nearly one-fifth of its more than 700 employees are based in the United States.[18]
- Aixtron SE was the target of a proposed acquisition by Grand Chip Investment GmbH, a German limited liability company, whose ultimate owners included Fujian Grand Chip Investment Fund LP and other Chinese investors, some of which have Chinese government ownership.
- The proposed acquisition was to have been funded in part by Sino IC Leasing Co., Ltd., a financing provider belonging to China IC Industry Investment Fund, a Chinese government-supported industrial investment fund established to promote the development of China's integrated circuit industry.
- In October 2016, the German Ministry of Economics withdrew a certificate of non-objection that it previously had granted regarding the acquisition of Germany-based Aixtron by FGC and announced that it was reopening its review based on security concerns communicated to the ministry by the US Government.[19]
- A statement from the Treasury Department stated that the administration blocked the purchase of the American portion of Aixtron's business because it posed a national security risk relating to "the military applications of the overall technical body of knowledge and experience of Aixtron."

[18] Paul Mozur (2016): Obama Moves to Block Chinese Acquisition of a German Chip Maker, *The New York Times*, December 12, 2016.

[19] Jeremy B. Zucker and Sven Schulte-Hillen (2016): Following CFIUS Recommendation, President Obama Blocks Chinese Acquisition of US-German Semiconductor Equipment Manufacturer, Dechert LLP, December 20, 2016.

Order of December 2, 2016

Regarding the Proposed Acquisition of a Controlling Interest in Aixtron SE by Grand Chip Investment GmbH by the authority vested in me as President by the Constitution and the laws of the United States, including Section 721 of the Defense Production Act of 1950, as amended (Section 721), 50 U.S.C. 4565,

Section 1. Findings. I hereby make the following findings:

(a) There is credible evidence that leads me to believe that: (1) Grand Chip Investment GmbH, a limited liability company organized under the laws of the Federal Republic of Germany (Grand Chip); (2) Grand Chip's parent companies Grand Chip Investment S.a.r.l., a company organized under the laws of the Grand Duchy of Luxembourg (GC Investment), and Fujian Grand Chip Investment Fund LP, a limited partnership organized under the laws of the People's Republic of China (Fujian Grand); and (3) Fujian Grand's partners, Mr. Zhendong Liu, a citizen of the People's Republic of China (Mr. Liu), and Xiamen Bohao Investment Co. Ltd., a company organized under the laws of the People's Republic of China (Xiamen Bohao and, together with Grand Chip, GC Investment, Fujian Grand, and Mr. Liu, the Purchasers), through exercising control of the US business of AIXTRON SE., a company organized under the laws of the Federal Republic of Germany (Aixtron), might take action that threatens to impair the national security of the United States. The US business of Aixtron consists of AIXTRON, Inc., a California corporation, the equity interests of AIXTRON, Inc., and any asset of Aixtron or AIXTRON, Inc. used in, or owned for the use in or benefit of, the activities in interstate commerce in the United States of AIXTRON, Inc., including without limitation any interest in any patents issued by, and any interest in any patent applications pending with, the United States Patent and Trademark Office (collectively, Aixtron US); and

(b) Provisions of law, other than Section 721 and the International Emergency Economic Powers Act (50 U.S.C. 1701 et seq.), do not, in my judgment, provide adequate and appropriate authority for me to protect the national security in this matter.

Sect. 2. Actions Ordered and Authorized. On the basis of the findings set forth in Section 1 of this order, considering the factors described in Subsection 721(f), as appropriate, and pursuant to my authority under applicable law, including Section 721, I hereby order that:

(a) The proposed acquisition of Aixtron US by the Purchasers is hereby prohibited, and any substantially equivalent transaction, whether effected directly or indirectly through the Purchasers' shareholders, partners, subsidiaries, or affiliates is prohibited.

(b) In order to effectuate this order, the Purchasers and Aixtron shall take all steps necessary to fully and permanently abandon the proposed acquisition of Aixtron US not later than 30 days after the date of this order, unless such date is extended by the Committee on Foreign Investment in the United States (CFIUS) for a period not to exceed 90 days, on such written conditions as CFIUS may require. Immediately upon completion of all steps necessary to terminate the proposed acquisition of Aixtron US, the Purchasers and Aixtron shall certify in writing to CFIUS that such termination has been effected in accordance with this order and that all steps necessary to fully and permanently abandon the proposed acquisition of Aixtron US have been completed.

(c) From the date of this order until the Purchasers and Aixtron provide a certification of termination of the proposed acquisition to CFIUS pursuant to subsection (b) of this section, the Purchasers and Aixtron shall certify to CFIUS on a weekly basis that they are in compliance with this order and include a description of efforts to permanently abandon the proposed acquisition of Aixtron US and a timeline for projected completion of remaining actions.

(d) Any transaction or other device entered into or employed for the purpose of, or with the effect of, avoiding or circumventing this order is prohibited.

(e) The Attorney General is authorized to take any steps necessary to enforce this order.

Sec. 3. Reservation. I hereby reserve my authority to issue further orders with respect to the Purchasers, Aixtron, or Aixtron US as shall in my judgment be necessary to protect the national security.

Sec. 4. Publication and Transmittal. (a) This order shall be published in the Federal Register.

(b) I hereby direct the Secretary of the Treasury to transmit a copy of this order to the appropriate parties named in Section 1 of this order.

THE WHITE HOUSE.

CHAPTER 4

M&A Policies Review Under the Competition Laws in the European Union

4.1 General

Although the Treaty of Rome does not contain any specific provision (Article) which deal with mergers and acquisitions, it provided some control to the EU Commission to control practices of dominant firms under Articles 86 and 87. The Treaty on the Functioning of the European Union ("TFEU"), prohibits two types of competition practices: (i) concentration and (ii) abuse of dominant position.

Under Article 3(2) the EU has exclusive competence in the following areas: (a) customs union; (b) the establishment of the competition rules necessary for the functioning of the internal market; (c) monetary policy for the Member States whose currency is the euro; (d) the conservation of marine biological resources under the common fisheries policy; and (e) common commercial policy.

The EU also has exclusive competence for the conclusion of an international agreement when its conclusion is provided for in a legislative act of the Union or is necessary to enable the Union to exercise its internal competence, or in so far as its conclusion may affect common rules or alter their scope. Competition law decisions are taken by the College of

F. I. Lessambo, *Mergers in the Global Markets*,
https://doi.org/10.1007/978-3-030-43558-5_4

Commissioners, reflecting the views of not only the Competition Commissioner, but of the other 27 Commissioners responsible for other policies.[1]

EU competition law is driven by the integration of the European market.[2] Mario Monti, the E.U. Competition Commissioner, stated that:

> Competition policy is also strictly connected with another of the fundamental objectives of the E.C. Treaty, namely the creation of the Single Market.[3]

The European courts have a greater role in merger matters administered by the European Commission than US courts do in cases administered by the FTC or DOJ.

A concentration is deemed to arise where a change of control on a lasting basis results from:

(a) the merger of two or more previously independent undertakings or parts of undertakings or
(b) the acquisition, by one or more persons already controlling at least one undertaking, or by one or more undertakings, whether by purchase of securities or assets, by contract or by any other means, of direct or indirect control of the whole or parts of one or more other undertakings.

According to Article 3(1) of the Merger Regulation, a concentration only covers operations where a change of control in the undertakings concerned occurs on a lasting basis. A concentration has a Community dimension where: (a) the combined aggregate worldwide turnover of all the undertakings concerned is more than EUR 5000 million; and (b) the aggregate Community-wide turnover of each of at least two of the undertakings concerned is more than EUR 250 million, unless each of

[1] Ariel Ezrachi (2015): Sponge, University of Oxford Centre for Competition Law and Policy, Working Paper CCLP (L) 42.

[2] Other objectives pursued include: the promotion of efficiency and consumer welfare, the protection of market structure and economic freedom.

[3] Mario Monti (2001): European Competition for the 21st Century, *Fordham International Law Journal*, Vol. 24, pp. 1602, 1604.

the undertakings concerned achieves more than two-thirds of its aggregate Community-wide turnover within one and the same Member State. Nonetheless, a concentration that does not meet the aforementioned thresholds would still have a Community dimension where:

(a) the combined aggregate worldwide turnover of all the undertakings concerned is more than EUR 2500 million;
(b) in each of at least three Member States, the combined aggregate turnover of all the undertakings concerned is more than EUR 100 million;
(c) in each of at least three Member States included for the purpose of point (b), the aggregate turnover of each of at least two of the undertakings concerned is more than EUR 25 million; and
(d) the aggregate Community-wide turnover of each of at least two of the undertakings concerned is more than EUR 100 million, unless each of the undertakings concerned achieves more than two-thirds of its aggregate Community-wide turnover within one and the same Member State.

Where the Commission finds that a notified concentration falls within the scope of this Regulation, it shall publish the fact of the notification, at the same time indicating the names of the undertakings concerned, their country of origin, the nature of the concentration and the economic sectors involved.

A concentration with a Community dimension or which is to be examined by the Commission will not be implemented either before its notification or until it has been declared compatible with the common market.

4.2 EU Core Competition Laws

The three core provisions are Article 101 (ex-Article 81 TEC), Article 102 (ex-Article 82 TEC), and Article 106 (ex-Article 86 TEC).

- Article 101(1) prohibits as incompatible with the internal market and declares void with the internal market: all agreements between undertakings, decisions by associations of undertakings and concerted practices which may affect trade between Member States and which have as their object or effect the prevention, restriction, or distortion of competition within the common market, and in particular those which:

(a) directly or indirectly fix purchase or selling prices or any other trading conditions;
(b) limit or control production, markets, technical development, or investment;
(c) share markets or sources of supply;
(d) apply dissimilar conditions to equivalent transactions with other trading parties, thereby placing them at a competitive disadvantage;
(e) make the conclusion of contracts subject to acceptance by the other parties of supplementary obligations which, by their nature or according to commercial usage, have no connection with the subject of such contracts.

However, under Article 101(3) any agreement or category of agreements between undertakings, any decision or category of decisions by associations of undertakings, any concerted practice or category of concerted practices, which contributes to improving the production or distribution of goods or to promoting technical or economic progress, while allowing consumers a fair share of the resulting benefit, would not be declared incompatible and void if the following requirements are met: the agreement does not (i) impose on the undertakings concerned restrictions which are not indispensable to the attainment of these objectives; (ii) afford such undertakings the possibility of eliminating competition in respect of a substantial part of the products in question.

- Article 102, which prohibits any abuse of dominant position states:

Any abuse by one or more undertakings of a dominant position within the internal market or in a substantial part of it shall be prohibited as incompatible with the internal market in so far as it may affect trade between the Member States.

Such abuse may, in particular, consist in:

(a) directly or indirectly imposing unfair purchase or selling prices or other unfair trading conditions;

(b) limiting production, markets, or technical development to the prejudice of consumers;
(c) applying dissimilar conditions to equivalent transactions with other trading parties, thereby placing them at a competitive disadvantage;
(d) making the conclusion of contracts subject to acceptance by the other parties of supplementary obligations which, by their nature or according to commercial usage, have no connection with the subject of such contracts.

- Article 106 provides that:

In the case of public undertakings and undertakings to which Member States grant special or exclusive rights, Member States shall neither enact nor maintain in force any measure contrary to the rules contained in the Treaties.

Undertakings entrusted with the operation of services of general economic interest or having the character of a revenue-producing monopoly shall be subject to the rules contained in the Treaties, in particular to the rules on competition, in so far as the application of such rules does not obstruct the performance, in law or in fact, of the particular tasks assigned to them. The development of trade must not be affected to such an extent as would be contrary to the interests of the Union.

One or more Member States may request the Commission to examine any concentration that does not have a Community dimension but affects trade between Member States and threatens to significantly affect competition within the territory of the Member State or States making the request. Such a request is made at most within 15 working days of the date on which the concentration was notified, or if no notification is required, otherwise made known to the Member State concerned.

4.3 The Notification Procedure

In the case of a merger within the meaning of Article 3(1)(a) of the EC Merger Regulation or the acquisition of joint control of an undertaking within the meaning of Article 3(1)(b) of the EC Merger Regulation, the notification is completed jointly by the parties to the merger or by those acquiring joint control, as the case may be. In case of the acquisition of a controlling interest in one undertaking by another, the acquirer must complete the notification. In the case of a public bid to acquire an undertaking, the bidder must complete the notification.

The notification of the concentration to the Commission is usually preceded by prenotification discussions in which the merging parties and the Commission's case team look over initial questions on the transaction and the relevant markets.

Each party completing the notification is responsible for the accuracy of the information which it provides. Each party provides an executive summary of the concentration, specifying the parties to the concentration, the nature of the concentration, the areas of activity of the notifying parties, the markets on which the concentration will have an impact (including the main affected markets), and the strategic and economic rationale for the concentration. The notifying parties can also request that an oral hearing be organized before the case team of the Commission, other Commission services, and interested third parties.

The notifying parties must provide the following:

- copies of the final or most recent versions of all documents bringing about the concentration, whether by agreement between the parties to the concentration, acquisition of a controlling interest or a public bid;
- in a public bid, a copy of the offer document; if it is unavailable at the time of notification, it should be submitted as soon as possible and not later than when it is posted to shareholders;
- copies of the most recent annual reports and accounts of all the parties to the concentration; and
- copies of all analyses, reports, studies, surveys, and any comparable documents prepared by or for any member(s) of the board of directors, or the supervisory board, or the other person(s) exercising similar functions (or to whom such functions have been delegated or entrusted), or the shareholders' meeting, for the purpose of assessing or analyzing the concentration with respect to market shares, competitive conditions, competitors (actual and potential), the rationale of the concentration, potential for sales growth or expansion into other product or geographic markets, and/or general market conditions.

4.3.1 Breach of the Standstill Obligation

The Commission considers breach of the standstill obligation to be an extremely serious offense and stated in the press release announcing its infringement decision that:

> This so-called standstill obligation constitutes a cornerstone of the EU merger control system... The early implementation of a concentration affects the structure of the market and may make it considerably more difficult... to restore effective competition... In order to avoid any permanent and irreparable damage to effective competition, companies are obliged to give prior notification of concentrations...and not to implement these concentrations before having received clearance... Any infringement of these obligations is serious.

- The Marine harvest Case[4]

- In December 2012, Marine Harvest purchased 48.5% of the shares in Morpol by way of a share purchase agreement with Morpol's largest shareholder.
- The transaction was completed without notification to the Commission.
- Morpol was listed on the Oslo stock exchange, and, in January 2013, Marine Harvest made a mandatory public offer for the remaining shares in Morpol.
- Following completion of this mandatory offer, Marine Harvest held 87.1% of the shares in Morpol.
- The transaction was notified to the Commission, and Marine Harvest informed the Commission that it would not exercise any voting rights or control over Morpol pursuant to the exception set forth by Article 7(2) EUMR.
- The Commission ultimately cleared the transaction (subject to conditions meant to protect competition in the market for the farming and processing of Scottish salmon).
- Nonetheless, it kept investigating the circumstances around the December 2012 transaction, and reached the conclusion that the

[4] Case COMP/M.6850 Marine Harvest/Morpol.

acquisition of the 48.5% shareholding had already conferred to Marine Harvest de facto control over Morpol.
- On July 23, 2014, consequently, the Commission imposed a fine of EUR 20 million against Marine Harvest; EUR 10 million for the failure of prior notification and EUR 10 million for breaching the standstill obligation.
- Marine Harvest appealed the fine before the EU General Court.

4.3.2 *Exception to the Standstill Obligation*

Article 7(2) EUMR provides:

- The Marine harvest Case(Appeal)[5]

- In its defense, Marine Harvest referred to Article 7(2) of the EUMR, which exempts, under certain conditions, "a public bid" or "a series of transactions in securities" from the standstill obligation.
- Marine Harvest raised a four-prong argument all tied up to Article 7(2).
- On October 26, 2017, the General Court dismissed all of Marine Harvest's arguments.
    - ➢ First, the General Court confirmed that by acquiring 48.5% of the shares in Morpol, Marine Harvest had completed a notifiable concentration in December 2012, before the transaction was formally notified. That is, the transaction was an acquisition of de facto control because Marine Harvest could expect a de facto majority of voting rights at Morpol's shareholders' meetings given the level of attendance in previous years.
    - ➢ Second, the General Court found that Marine Harvest could not rely on the exception in Art. 7(2) EUMR. Morpol was a listed company. But the December 2012 acquisition was a private purchase from a single seller. The mandatory public bid was launched only afterwards. The December 2012 acquisition and the public bid could not be deemed to be a "series

[5] Case T-704/14 Marine Harvest vs. Commission.

of transactions in securities" that constituted a single transaction, either, because the December 2012 acquisition already constituted, by itself, an acquisition of control. The fact that Marine Harvest was committed to not exercising the voting rights until after the clearance decision from the Commission did not change the outcome of the analysis. It could merely be taken into account as a "mitigating circumstance" when determining the appropriate level of the fine.

- Third, the General Court also confirmed the fine imposed by the Commission. The level of the fine was justified, in its view, because there had been serious doubts whether the transaction could be cleared and because of the potential damages for competition resulting from the early implementation. The General Court noted that despite refraining from exercising its voting rights, Marine Harvest internalized a large share of Morpol's profits, and it may have played a role in the resignation of the CEO of the Morpol group.
- Fourth, the General Court confirmed the negligent character of the infringement because the applicant "did not exercise all the diligence required of a normally experienced person" and ruled out any excusable error. Assuming that this was the first time a company has been fined for breaching notification and standstill obligations in relation to the exception contained in Article 7(2) EUMR, the Court considered that there was no need for the European Commission to be particularly lenient toward Marine Harvest.

4.4 Commission Examination

4.4.1 Relevant Geographic Market

Market shares and concentration levels provide useful first indications of the market structure and of the competitive importance of both the merging parties and their competitors. The relevant geographic market comprises the area in which the undertakings concerned are involved in the supply and demand of products or services, in which the conditions of competition are sufficiently homogeneous and which can be distinguished from neighboring areas because the conditions of competition are appreciably different in those areas. The definition of the relevant market in both its product and geographic dimensions allows the identification of the suppliers and the customers/consumers active in that market. On that basis, the total market size and market shares for each supplier can be calculated on the basis of their sales of the relevant products in the relevant area.

Normally, the Commission uses current market shares in its competitive analysis. However, current market shares may be adjusted to reflect reasonably certain future changes, for instance in the light of exit, entry, or expansion. Post-merger market shares are calculated on the assumption that the post-merger combined market share of the merging parties is the sum of their pre-merger market shares. Historic data may be used if market shares have been volatile, for instance when the market is characterized by large, lumpy orders. Changes in historic market shares may provide useful information about the competitive process and the likely future importance of the various competitors, for instance, by indicating whether firms have been gaining or losing market shares. In any event, the Commission interprets market shares in the light of likely market conditions, for instance, if the market is highly dynamic in character and if the market structure is unstable due to innovation or growth.

The overall concentration level in a market may also provide useful information about the competitive situation. In order to measure concentration levels, the Commission often applies the Herfindahl–Hirschman Index (HHI). The HHI is calculated by summing the squares of the individual market shares of all the firms in the market. The HHI gives proportionately greater weight to the market shares of the larger firms. Although it is best to include all firms in the calculation, lack of information about very small firms may not be important because such firms do not affect the HHI significantly. While the absolute level of the HHI can give an initial indication of the competitive pressure in the market post-merger, the change in the HHI (known as the "delta") is a useful proxy for the change in concentration directly brought about by the merger.

- Market share levels

According to well-established case law, very large market shares—50% or more—may, in themselves, constitute evidence of the existence of a dominant market position (20). However, smaller competitors may act as a sufficient constraining influence if, for example, they have the ability and incentive to increase their supplies. A merger involving a firm whose market share will remain below 50% after the merger may also raise competition concerns in view of other factors such as the strength and number of competitors, the presence of capacity constraints or the extent to which the products of the merging parties are close substitutes. The Commission has thus in several cases considered mergers resulting in firms holding market shares between 40 and 50%, and in some cases below 40%, to lead to the creation or the strengthening of a dominant position.

Concentrations which, by reason of the limited market share of the undertakings concerned, are not liable to impede effective competition may be presumed to be compatible with the common market. Without prejudice to Articles 81 and 82 of the Treaty, an indication to this effect exists, in particular, where the market shares of the undertakings concerned does not exceed 25% either in the common market or in a substantial part of it.

- HHI levels

The Commission is unlikely to identify horizontal competition concerns in a market with a post-merger HHI below 1000. Such markets normally do not require extensive analysis.

The Commission is also unlikely to identify horizontal competition concerns in a merger with a post-merger HHI between 1000 and 2000 and a delta below 250, or a merger with a post-merger HHI above 2000 and a delta below 150, except where special circumstances such as, for instance, one or more of the following factors are present:

(a) A merger involves a potential entrant or a recent entrant with a small market share;
(b) One or more merging parties are important innovators in ways not reflected in market shares;
(c) There are significant cross-shareholdings among the market participants;
(d) One of the merging firms is a maverick firm with a high likelihood of disrupting coordinated conduct;

(e) Indications of past or ongoing coordination, or facilitating practices, are present;
(f) One of the merging parties has a pre-merger market share of 50% of more.

Each of these HHI levels, in combination with the relevant deltas, may be used as an initial indicator of the absence of competition concerns. However, they do not give rise to a presumption of either the existence or the absence of such concerns.

4.4.2 Countervailing Buyer Power

The competitive pressure on a supplier is not only exercised by competitors but can also come from its customers. Even firms with very high market shares may not be in a position, post-merger, to significantly impede effective competition, in particular by acting to an appreciable extent independently of their customers, if the latter possess countervailing buyer power. Countervailing buyer power in this context should be understood as the bargaining strength that the buyer has vis-à-vis the seller in commercial negotiations due to its size, its commercial significance to the seller and its ability to switch to alternative suppliers.

The Commission considers, when relevant, to what extent customers will be in a position to counter the increase in market power that a merger would otherwise be likely to create. One source of countervailing buyer power would be if a customer could credibly threaten to resort, within a reasonable timeframe, to alternative sources of supply should the supplier decide to increase prices (80) or to otherwise deteriorate the quality or the conditions of delivery. This would be the case if the buyer could immediately switch to other suppliers, credibly threaten to vertically integrate into the upstream market or to sponsor upstream expansion or entry for instance by persuading a potential entrant to enter by committing to placing large orders with this company. It is more likely that large and sophisticated customers will possess this kind of countervailing buyer power than smaller firms in a fragmented industry. A buyer may also exercise countervailing buying power by refusing to buy other products produced by the supplier or, particularly in the case of durable goods, delaying purchases.

In some cases, it may be important to pay particular attention to the incentives of buyers to utilize their buyer power. For example, a downstream firm may not wish to make an investment in sponsoring new entry if the benefits of such entry in terms of lower input costs could also be reaped by its competitors.

4.4.3 Efficiencies

Corporate reorganizations in the form of mergers may be in line with the requirements of dynamic competition and are capable of increasing the competitiveness of industry, thereby improving the conditions of growth and raising the standard of living in the Community. It is possible that efficiencies brought about by a merger counteract the effects on competition and in particular the potential harm to consumers that it might otherwise have. In order to assess whether a merger would significantly impede effective competition, in particular through the creation or the strengthening of a dominant position, within the meaning of Article 2(2) and (3) of the Merger Regulation, the Commission performs an overall competitive appraisal of the merger. In making this appraisal, the Commission takes into account the factors mentioned in Article 2(1), including the development of technical and economic progress provided that it is to the consumers' advantage and does not form an obstacle to competition.

Put differently, efficiency is considered as an element of the restriction of competition, and the guidelines on horizontal mergers published by the Commission point equally to the possibility that efficiency gains will offset anticompetitive effects.[6] However, the measurement of efficiency gains and its effects on competition are fair for being accepted outside the circle of competition economists.

- The Sun Alliance case

  - Sun Alliance Group plc (Sun) and Royal Insurance Holdings plc (Royal) entered into a full merger within the meaning of Article 3(1)a of the Merger Regulation.

[6] Jurgen Basedoq (2007): The Modernization of European Competition Law: A Story of Unfinished Concepts, *Texas International Law Review*, Vol. 42: 429, p. 435.

- Sun and Royal merged their worldwide activities by means of an exchange of shares.
- Sun's principal activity consisted of the life and nonlife insurance. The life insurance side of the business involved products such as life insurance, pensions, annuities, and permanent health insurance. Sun's nonlife business, which covered products such as commercial property, household, and motor insurance, comprises both UK and overseas operations.
- Royal was also a composite insurer which provided all major classes of insurance and related financial services. Overseas activities were widely spread, with substantial businesses in the United States and Canada and European activities concentrated in Portugal, Spain, and Italy.
- In its analysis of the proposed merger, the Commission looks (i) whether the merger constituted concentration under Article 3(1) of the Merger Regulations; (ii) whether the merger had a Community dimension; and (iii) whether the merger was compatible with the common market. The Commission found the following:

  (i) The merger of Sun and Royal constituted a concentration within the meaning of Article 3(1)a of the Merger Regulation.

  (ii) The aggregate Community-wide turnover of each of the two undertakings amounted the same year to more than 250 million ECU. The two companies did not achieve more than two-thirds of their aggregate Community-wide turnover within one and the same Member State; although the activities of both undertakings were centered in the United Kingdom, Sun did not achieve two-thirds of its aggregate Community-wide turnover in this country in 1995. Therefore, the concentration had a Community dimension.

  (iii) The assessment of the compatibility involved several steps from the relevant market products, the geographic reference to the competitiveness assessment.

  ➢ The Commission made a distinction between the insurance activities and reinsurance to exclude the latter from its analysis. It found that the insurance side did not raise serious doubts as to its compatibility with the common market.

- ➢ The Commission also determined that as far as life and nonlife insurance were concerned, geographical reference markets seemed to be mainly national in view of the established market structures. That the need for adequate distribution channels, fiscal constraints, and national systems of regulatory supervision was the province of Member State.
- ➢ In the life insurance sector, the activities of both Sun and Royal were concentrated almost exclusively in the U.K., where for most products combined market shares were less than 5%, and did not for any product exceed 15%. The main impact of the concentration was found in the nonlife insurance sector where significant overlaps in the parties business lead to combined market shares of more than 15% in specific sectors.
- ➢ The Commission found that there were strong competitors present in all these sectors, such as Commercial Union, General Accident, Eagle Star, Legal and General, Guardian, and so on. That, there would seem to be some degree of supply-side substitutability in the nonlife insurance sector.
- ➢ Therefore, the Commission decided not to oppose the notified operation and declared it compatible with the common market and with the functioning of the EEA Agreement.

4.4.4 *Entry*

When entering a market is sufficiently easy, a merger is unlikely to pose any significant anticompetitive risk. Therefore, entry analysis constitutes an important element of the overall competitive assessment. For entry to be considered a sufficient competitive constraint on the merging parties, it must be shown to be likely, timely and sufficient to deter or defeat any potential anticompetitive effects of the merger.

4.4.5 *Failing Firm*

The Commission may decide that an otherwise problematic merger is nevertheless compatible with the common market if one of the merging parties is a failing firm. The basic requirement is that the deterioration of the competitive structure that follows the merger cannot be said to be caused by the merger. This will arise where the competitive structure of the market would deteriorate to at least the same extent in the absence of the merger. The Commission considers the following three criteria to be especially relevant for the application of a "failing firm defense." First, the allegedly failing firm would in the near future be forced out of the market because of financial difficulties if not taken over by another undertaking. Second, there is no less anticompetitive alternative purchase than the notified merger. Third, in the absence of a merger, the assets of the failing firm would inevitably exit the market.

It is for the notifying parties to provide in due time all the relevant information necessary to demonstrate that the deterioration of the competitive structure that follows the merger is not caused by the merger.

4.5 Vertical and Conglomerate Mergers

Non-horizontal mergers are generally less likely to significantly impede effective competition than horizontal mergers. First, unlike horizontal mergers, vertical or conglomerate mergers do not entail the loss of direct competition between the merging firms in the same relevant market. Second, vertical and conglomerate mergers provide substantial scope for efficiencies. A characteristic of vertical mergers and certain conglomerate mergers is that the activities and/or the products of the companies involved are complementary to each other. The Commission is unlikely to find concern in non-horizontal mergers, be it of a coordinated or of a non-coordinated nature, where the market shares post-merger of the new entity in each of the markets concerned is below 30% (3) and the post-merger HHI is below 2000. In practice, the Commission will not extensively investigate such mergers, except where special circumstances such as, for instance, one or more of the following factors are present: (a) merger involves a company that is likely to expand significantly in the near future, e.g., because of a recent innovation; (b) there are significant cross-shareholdings or cross-directorships among the market participants; (c) one of the merging firms is a firm with a high likelihood of disrupting coordinated conduct; and (d) indications of past or ongoing coordination, or facilitating practices, are present.

4.5.1 *Vertical Mergers*

The Commission will consider both the possible anticompetitive effects arising from vertical mergers and the possible pro-competitive effects stemming from efficiencies substantiated by the parties. A merger is said to result in foreclosure where actual or potential rivals' access to supplies or markets is hampered or eliminated as a result of the merger, thereby reducing these companies' ability and/or incentive to compete. Such foreclosure may discourage entry or expansion of rivals or encourage their exit. Foreclosure thus can be found even if the foreclosed rivals are not forced to exit the market: It is sufficient that the rivals are disadvantaged and consequently led to compete less effectively. Such foreclosure is regarded as anticompetitive where the merging companies and, possibly, some of its competitors as well are as a result able to profitably increase the price charged to consumers. Two forms of foreclosure can be distinguished. The first is where the merger is likely to raise the costs of downstream rivals by restricting their access to an important input (input foreclosure). The second is where the merger is likely to foreclose upstream rivals by restricting their access to a sufficient customer base (customer foreclosure).

4.5.2 *Conglomerate Mergers*

Conglomerate mergers are mergers between firms that are in a relationship which is neither purely horizontal (as competitors in the same relevant market) nor vertical (as supplier and customer). In practice, the focus is on mergers between companies that are active in closely related markets (2) Whereas it is acknowledged that conglomerate mergers in the majority of circumstances will not lead to any competition problems, in certain specific cases there may be harm to competition. In its assessment, the Commission will consider both the possible anticompetitive effects arising from conglomerate mergers and the possible pro-competitive effects stemming from efficiencies substantiated by the parties.

The main concern in the context of conglomerate mergers is that of foreclosure. The combination of products in related markets may confer on the merged entity the ability and incentive to leverage (1) a strong market position from one market to another by means of tying or bundling or other exclusionary practices (2). Tying and bundling as such are common practices that often have no anticompetitive consequences.

Companies engage in tying and bundling in order to provide their customers with better products or offerings in cost-effective ways. Nevertheless, in certain circumstances, these practices may lead to a reduction in actual or potential rivals' ability or incentive to compete. This may reduce the competitive pressure on the merged entity allowing it to increase prices.

In assessing the likelihood of such a scenario, the Commission examines, first, whether the merged firm would have the ability to foreclose its rivals, second, whether it would have the economic incentive to do so and, third, whether a foreclosure strategy would have a significant detrimental effect on competition, thus causing harm to consumers (3). In practice, these factors are often examined together as they are closely intertwined.

- Ability to foreclose

In order to be able to foreclose competitors, the new entity must have a significant degree of market power, which does not necessarily amount to dominance, in one of the markets concerned. The effects of bundling or tying can only be expected to be substantial when at least one of the merging parties' products is viewed by many customers as particularly important and there are few relevant alternatives for that product, e.g., because of product differentiation (1) or capacity constraints on the part of rivals. For foreclosure to be a potential concern it must be the case that there is a large common pool of customers for the individual products concerned. The more customers tend to buy both products (instead of only one of the products), the more demand for the individual products may be affected through bundling or tying. Such a correspondence in purchasing behavior is more likely to be significant when the products in question are complementary. The foreclosure effects of bundling and tying are likely to be more pronounced in industries where there are economies of scale and the demand pattern at any given point in time has dynamic implications for the conditions of supply in the market in the future. Notably, where a supplier of complementary goods has market power in one of the products (product A), the decision to bundle or tie may result in reduced sales by the nonintegrated suppliers of the complementary good (product B). It can also be noted that the scope for foreclosure tends to be smaller where the merging parties cannot commit to making their tying or bundling strategy a lasting one, for example through technical tying or bundling which is costly to reverse.

- Incentive to foreclose

The incentive to foreclose rivals through bundling or tying depends on the degree to which this strategy is profitable. The merged entity faces a trade-off between the possible costs associated with bundling or tying its products and the possible gains from expanding market shares in the market(s) concerned or, as the case may be, being able to raise the price in those market(s) due to its market power.

- Overall likely impact on price and choice

Foreclosure practices may deter entry by potential competitors. They may do so for a specific market by reducing sales prospects for potential rivals in that market to a level below the minimum viable scale. In the case of complementary products, deterring entry in one market through bundling or tying may also allow the merged entity to deter entry in another market if the bundling or tying forces potential competitors to enter both product markets at the same time rather than entering only one of them or entering them sequentially. The latter may have a significant impact in particular in those industries where the demand pattern at any given point in time has dynamic implications for the conditions of supply in the market in the future.

4.6 Remedies

Where a proposed concentration threatens to significantly impede effective competition the most effective way to maintain effective competition, apart from prohibition, is to create the conditions for the emergence of a new competitive entity or for the strengthening of existing competitors via divestiture by the merging parties.

4.7 M&A Review Under National Security Laws in the EU

The European merger review system was established by a European Council regulation, officially referred to as the "EC Merger Regulation." As has become the international standard, the EC requires prenotification for mergers meeting certain thresholds for turnover. At the EC level, enforcement is handled by the Directorate General for Competition ("DG-Comp"). For those mergers within the ambit of the Commission's jurisdiction, Article 21(4) EUMR does, however, allow Member States to take appropriate measures to protect legitimate public interests that are not taken into consideration under the EUMR, provided those measures are compatible with the general principles and other provisions of EU law. Article 21(4) of the EUMR provides three legitimate interests:

- public security (Member States are permitted to take measures based on public security grounds, including interests related to the defense policy);
- plurality of the media (measures may be taken to ensure plurality of the media to allow Member States to ensure diversity of opinion); and
- prudential rules (rules to protect "prudential interests" are of relevance in the area of financial services).

In addition to the aforementioned, the Commission may permit national intervention on other legitimate interest grounds, wherever deemed appropriate.

Mergers not meeting EC thresholds may still be subject to review by the competition authorities of an individual Member State. While the EC does not conduct its own national security review, several provisions in the TFEU and EC Merger Regulation contemplate Member States conducting such a review. Within the TFEU, Article 346 provides two blanket exceptions to all provisions of the treaty. First, Member States cannot be made to disclose confidential information that, by the Member State's own determination, bears on national security. Second, Article 346(1)(b) of the TFEU provides:

> Any Member State may take such measures as it considers necessary for the protection of the essential interests of its security which are connected

with the production of or trade in arms, munitions and war material; such measures shall not adversely affect the conditions of competition in the common market regarding products which are not intended for specifically military purposes.

The EC Merger Regulation confirms this exception and expands the scope of interests which enable Member States to raise an exception to EC action.

Rather than use the "essential interests" standard of the TFEU, the EC Merger Regulation adopts the language "legitimate interests." It seems clear that an interest can be "legitimate" without in any way approaching the level of being "essential," and thus the Merger Regulation provides much more leeway than is required under the treaty. Further, the EC Merger Regulation enumerates "public security" as a legitimate interest, which again seems to be a relaxation of the strictly military terminology used in the TFEU.

Finally, Article 21 also provides a catchall provision that basically allows Member States to attempt to raise anything in the "public interest" as a reason to intervene in an EC merger clearance. This is the most generous provision yet, because the public can certainly have a number of interests that do not even rise to the threshold of "legitimacy." However, in the event that a Member State does raise an exception under the "public interest" catchall provision, the Commission has the discretion to determine whether it is "compatible with the general principles and other provisions of Community law" before allowing the Member State to take action on those grounds.

4.7.1 EUMR Approved Cases Under the National Security Concerns

- Thomson-CSF/Racal[7]

- Thomson was a French company active in professional electronics and defense systems. It was jointly controlled by Thomson SA (a holding company wholly owned by the French State, and also having interests in consumer electronics) and by Alcatel (active in communications, transportation, and energy infrastructure).

[7] Case COMP/M.1858 Thomson-CSF/Racal(II).

- Racal was a UK-based company active in defense and industrial electronics, and in transportation services.
- Thomson made a recommended cash offer for Racal's entire issued share capital with the intent to acquire sole control of Racal.
- The combined aggregate worldwide turnover of the parties to the concentration exceeded EUR 5000 million in 1998 and each of the undertakings concerned had a Community-wide turnover of more than EUR 250 million.
- Two sectors were covered: (a) Civil sector and (b) defense electronics.

(a) Civil sector

- Both Thomson and Racal have activities in the following areas: (i) air traffic management systems, (ii) satellite communication systems, (iii) navigation and mission computers for helicopters, (iv) cellular base-station antennas, (v) supply of telecommunication systems and services to the rail industry (vi) transportation telematic activities, (vii) information systems security, and (viii) payment and card-related products.
- The relevant geographic markets were: (i) Air traffic management systems (ATMs), (ii) Satellite communication systems (Satcoms), (iii) Navigation and mission computers for helicopters, (iv) Cellular base-station antennas, (v) Supply of telecommunications systems and services to the rail industry, (vi) Transportation telematics activities, (vii) Information systems security (ISS), and (viii) Payment and card-related products.

(b) Defense electronics

- Both Thomson and Racal were active in defense electronics. They operated both at the prime contractor level, where they offered military communication systems, military command, control and information systems, airborne radars, electronic warfare, and ground-based systems; and also at the subcontractor level, where they supply defense electronics equipment or subsystems to the systems prime contractors.

- The relevant product markets for that sector included: (i) Military communications, (ii) Command, control and information systems, (iii) Airborne radars, (iv) Electronic warfare (EW), (v) Ground-based systems (GBS).
- It is not necessary to further delineate the relevant geographic markets for defense electronics, as in all alternative market definitions considered, effective competition would not be significantly impeded in the EEA or any substantial part of that area.
- The EU Commission found that there was no indication that the elimination of the competition between Thomson and Racal could create or strengthen a dominant position, because a number of actual competitors and of potential entrants, such as BAE Systems, EADS, Lockheed Martin or Raytheon, can provide effective competition to the merged entity. That there was no indication that the operation could create competition concerns on the other markets, where the parties will remain subject to the competition from other prime contractors, such as BAE Systems, Raytheon, Lockheed Martin, or EADS.
- Thus, the EU Commission concluded that the proposed concentration did not create or strengthen a dominant position in defense electronics markets as a result of which effective competition would be significantly impeded in the EEA or any substantial part of that area.

4.7.2 National Security Interests in the UK

The Competition Act of 1998 and the Enterprise Act of 2002[8] brought the UK more into line with the European system of antitrust enforcement. The Enterprise Act of 2002 has created a new Competition Appeals Tribunal to review decisions by the competition agencies and the sectoral regulators. Currently, the UK Government has adopted the Enterprise and Regulatory Reform Act of 2013, which merges its two antitrust agencies into a new Competition and Markets Authority, effective since 2014.

In mergers raising certain public interest considerations, the Secretary of State for Business, Innovation and Skills may intervene and determine

[8] Enterprise Act, Sections 42–70.

whether or not to refer a merger to the Competition Commission and to take the ultimate decision in respect of mergers when defined public interest considerations are potentially relevant. There are three categories of public interest cases: (i) public interest; (ii) special public interest; and (iii) legitimate interests.

4.7.2.1 *Types of National Interests*

- Public interest

The UK Enterprise Act of 2002 enables the Secretary of State to intervene when he or she considers that one or more of the public interest considerations specified in the Act is or may be relevant to the consideration of a merger. Presently, the specified public interest considerations are:

- national security (including public security);
- the interests of maintaining the stability of the UK financial system; and
- the need for:
  - accurate presentation of news in newspapers;
  - free expression of opinion in newspapers;
  - a sufficient plurality of views in newspapers in each market for newspapers in the UK or a part of the UK to the extent that it is reasonable and practicable;
  - a sufficient plurality of persons with control of the media enterprises serving every different audience in the UK, or in a particular area or locality of the UK (the "plurality test");
  - the availability throughout the UK of a wide range of broadcasting which (taken as a whole) is both of high quality and calculated to appeal to a wide variety of tastes and interests; and
  - persons carrying on media enterprises, and for those with control of such enterprises, to have a genuine commitment to the attainment in relation to broadcasting of the standards and objectives set out in Section 319 of the Communications Act 2003.

The Secretary of State can modify the list of public interest considerations, to specify a new consideration or to remove or amend an existing consideration. In all circumstances the CC will consider whether:

(a) A relevant merger situation has been created or arrangements are in progress or contemplation that will lead to a relevant merger situation; and, if so,
(b) Whether the creation of the relevant merger situation operates, or may be expected to operate, against the public interest (the public interest test).

The factors that the CC must take into account when answering the public interest test vary according to the reference. Some references require the Competition Commission to consider the separate question of whether the creation of the relevant merger situation may be expected to result in an SLC. In these cases, the CC must answer the public interest test-taking account of any SLC and the relevant public interest consideration. If the CC finds that the merger is against the public interest, it then must consider appropriate remedial solutions.

- Special public interest

Special public interest cases concern mergers which may be referred to the Competition Commission on public interest grounds when the normal jurisdictional thresholds relating to turnover or share of supply in the Act are not satisfied. The category comprises:

(1) Certain media mergers

In respect of media mergers, a special merger situation is created if either:

(a) in relation to the supply of newspapers of any description, at least one-quarter of all the newspapers of that description which were supplied in the UK, or in a substantial part of it, were supplied by the person or persons by whom one of the enterprises concerned was carried on; or

(b) in relation to the provision of broadcasting of any description, at least one-quarter of all broadcasting of that description provided in the UK, or in a substantial part of it, was provided by the person or persons by whom one of the enterprises concerned was carried on.

The CC will have regard to both the range and the number of persons with control of media enterprises. The CC will also have regard to the degree of control exercised by one enterprise over another, including whether the extent and level of control are increased as a result of the merger. Where control is less than complete, the CC will consider whether in practice it would enable the controlling enterprise to dominate the policy and the output of the controlled enterprise. Where appropriate, the CC may distinguish between the plurality of persons with control of media enterprises and the implications of that plurality for the range of information and views made available to audiences.

(2) Mergers involving government contractors

In respect of mergers involving a government contractor, a special merger situation is created if:

(a) at least one of the enterprises concerned was carried on in the UK or in a substantial part of it, by, or under the control of, a body corporate incorporated in the UK and
(b) a person carrying on one or more of the enterprises concerned was a relevant government contractor.

In special merger cases raising public interest considerations, the Competition Commission must answer the following questions:

(a) Whether a special merger situation has been created (or arrangements for such a situation are in progress or contemplation) and, if so,
(b) Whether the creation of that situation operates (or may be expected to operate) against the public interest

If the Competition Commission finds that the merger operates against the public interest, it must consider whether remedial action is appropriate. However, the Competition Commission will not apply the SLC test but will decide the public interest question taking into account only the consideration mentioned in the reference.

- Legitimate interest

The competition assessment of the merger in this category of case remains the responsibility of the European Commission. However, the Enterprise Act allows the Secretary of State to intervene when the Secretary of State believes that one or more public interest considerations are relevant. The public interest grounds on which the Secretary of State may intervene are limited to those listed in Section 58 (other than the interest of maintaining the stability of the UK financial system, which is expressly stated not to be a consideration for the purposes of intervention under the ECMR).

4.7.2.2 Procedures in National Interests

In the three cases of national interests, the Secretary of State can issue a notice to require the office of fair trading to investigate the merger and provide a report. The Secretary of State is required to accept the OFT's findings on whether there is a "relevant merger situation" and, where appropriate, competition matters including the description of undertakings the OFT considers are appropriate in lieu of a reference.

4.7.2.3 Decision of the Secretary of State

On receipt of the CC's report, the Secretary of State has 30 working days in which to make a decision on the questions the CC had to decide. In public interest cases, the Secretary of State must accept the CC's decision on whether there is a relevant merger situation and whether that merger results in an SLC. In special public interest cases, the Secretary of State must accept the CC's decision on whether there is a special merger situation. In mergers with a "Community dimension," the Secretary of State must accept the CC's decision on whether there is a "European relevant merger situation."

In all three categories of cases, when deciding whether the merger is against the public interest, the Secretary of State is not bound by the

CC's views on the public interest test, having discretion in relation to the public interest consideration. The Secretary of State also has discretion when considering whether and which remedies are necessary to address the adverse public interest effects. If the Secretary of State decides that the merger is against the public interest, he or she has the power to take remedial action. In public interest cases, if the Secretary of State decides that the public interest issue is not relevant, the CC then decides how to remedy any competition issue identified.

4.7.3 National Security in Germany

In Germany, Public takeovers are overseen by the German Federal Financial Supervisory Authority (Bundesanstalt für Finanzdienstleistungsaufsicht "BaFin"). Under the Foreign Trade Act and the Foreign Trade Ordinance, the Federal Ministry for Economic Affairs and Energy has the authority to review (i) the acquisition of 25% or more of the voting rights in a domestic business by an acquirer domiciled outside the territory of the European Union or the European Free Trade Association and (ii) the acquisition by non-German companies of 25% or more of the voting rights in domestic companies that operate in industries sensitive to national security (primarily the weapons industry and encryption companies).

To endanger the German national security interest, the transaction must either affect material legal interests, or substantive issues regarding national and international security.[9] German laws do not define the concept of "national security interest" rather the legislature explicitly referred to Articles 46 and 58 of the Treaty Establishing the European Community (EC Treaty), where similar terms are used as exceptions to the freedom to provide services or form an establishment in another Member State.

The reviewing authority may prohibit, or may impose conditions on, the transaction within certain deadlines to the extent required to safeguard German public order or security. The parties must file with the Ministry prior to entering into binding agreements or announcing the transaction. If the Ministry prohibits the transaction, the parties must

[9] The following sectors are deemed of national interest: the telecommunication sector, electricity sector, energy and water supply sector, and other services of strategic importance.

abandon such a transaction. On the reverse, if the Ministry does not prohibit the transaction, it may still issue orders imposing several conditions upon the transaction.

4.7.3.1 The Review Process

The parties are under no obligation to make any filings and they are entitled to proceed with the transaction without clearance. Thus, any purchase agreement signed without clearance is deemed valid until prohibition order by the authority. The national security interest review process in Germany is conducted in two steps:

(1) the first step if the review is conducted within a period of a period not exceeding three months, starting from the purchase agreement and
(2) the second step two months (maximum) starting upon receipt of all information requested by the Ministry from the foreign buyer.

If the Ministry is of the opinion that the transaction endangers public order or security of the Federal Republic of Germany, it is entitled—with the consent of the German Government and within the two-month period—to prohibit the transaction or to issue orders in connection with the transaction. However, if the MET does not issue any prohibition or other order within those two months, the acquisition can no longer be restricted.

4.7.4 National Security in France

French regulation defines foreign investments subject to the prior authorization procedure when made in strategic sectors as follows:

- A transaction as a result of which a non-EU investor (i) acquires the control (within the meaning of art. L. 233-3 of the commercial code) (ii) acquires all or part of a business (branche d'activité), or (iii) crosses the threshold of 33.33 percent of the share capital, of a company whose registered office is located in France.
- A transaction as a result of which an EU investor (i) acquires the control (within the meaning of art. L. 233-3 of the commercial code) or

(ii) acquires all or part of a business of a company whose registered office is located in France.

- A transaction as a result of which a French investor under foreign control acquires all or part of a business of a company whose registered office is located in France.

On May 14, 2014, the Minister of Economy issued a decree amending the articles of the law that inter alia regulates foreign investment. The decree amends the list of activities subject to review for foreign investors equipment, services, and products that are essential to safeguard national interests in the areas of public order, public security, and national defense. Additional sectors cover in the decree include energy, transport, water, public health, and telecommunications. The scope of the prior authorization is extended to foreign investments in "activities relating to equipment, products or services, including those relating to the safety and the proper functioning of facilities and equipment, essential to guarantee the French national interests in terms of public policy, public security or national defense, as listed below:

- Integrity, security and continuity of the supply of electricity, gas, oil or other source of energy;
- Integrity, security and continuity of the water supply in accordance with the standards laid down in the interest of public health;
- Integrity, security and continuity of the operation of transportation networks and services;
- Integrity, security and continuity of the operation of electronic communication networks and services;
- Integrity, security and continuity of the operation of an installation, facility or structure of vital importance within the meaning of articles L. 1332-1 and L. 1332-2 of the Defense Code;
- Protection of the public health."

Soon after its adoption, the 2014-479 Decret (known as "the Decret Alstom") was submitted to the EU Commission for review. By way of a letter dated June 19, 2014, the EU Commission stated that though the Decret constituted a restriction to the free movement of capital and the freedom of establishment, its objectives were such as to be justified under Articles 52, 65, and 346 TFEU.

4.7.4.1 The Review Process

Foreign investors must submit a formal application for prior authorization to the French Minister of the Economy. The Ministry has two months from the date of receipt of a full and complete formal application for authorization to render its decision. The Minister of the Economy may impose certain conditions on the foreign investor to ensure that the contemplated transaction will not adversely affect public policy, public safety, or national security. Alternatively, the Minister of the Economy may refuse to authorize the contemplated transaction if adverse effects cannot be remedied. If the Minister of the Economy fails to render a decision authorization is deemed to have been granted.

To take the additional strategic sectors into account, the decree has added that such conditions may also aim at guarantying "the integrity, security and continuity of the operations of an installation, facility or structure of vital importance within the meaning of articles L. 1332-1 and L. 1332-2 of the Defense Code or of any transportation and electronic communication networks and services, or the protection of the public health."

4.7.5 National Security in Italy

In Italy, the "Strategic Sector Act" of 2012 grants the government the power (i) to veto any foreign investment affecting the safety of the Italian national and international defense, and to block any direct or indirect purchase of Italian assets that would enable or jeopardize the National Security Sector and (ii) to veto or block any foreign investment in Italian strategic industries, such as the Energy, Transportation, and Communications Sector. As to strategic sectors, the Italian Government may exercise the Special Powers described only vis-à-vis non-EU investors.

4.7.5.1 Procedure

Foreign investors must notify the Italian Government. The transaction is considered automatically approved, unless the government exercises its veto rights within 15 days. Concerning any purchase of Italian assets, the foreign investors must notify the Italian Government within 10 days, and the purchase is considered approved unless the government vetoes it within 15 days as of the day of the notice.

4.7.5.2 *Case Study: 50/50 Joint Venture (H3G) Between CK Hutchison Holdings (a Listed Hong Kong-Based Conglomerate) and VimpelCom Ltd.*

Facts:

- CK Hutchison is a multinational conglomerate headquartered in Hong Kong and listed on the Hong Kong Stock Exchange Limited. It operates in over 50 countries. CK Hutchison has five core businesses: ports and related services, retail, infrastructure, energy, and telecommunications. The telecommunications division includes mobile and fixed-line operations in Hong Kong and Macau, mobile operations in Indonesia, Vietnam, Sri Lanka, and Europe, mobile operations in Austria, Denmark, Ireland, Italy, Sweden, and the United Kingdom.
- VimpelCom, headquartered in Amsterdam, is one of the world's largest integrated telecommunications services operators providing voice and data services through a range of traditional and broadband mobile and fixed technologies in Russia, Italy, Ukraine, Kazakhstan, Uzbekistan, Tajikistan, Armenia, Georgia, Kyrgyzstan, Laos, Algeria, Bangladesh, Pakistan, and Zimbabwe.
- On August 6, 2015, CK Hutchison Holdings Ltd. ("CK Hutchison"), parent company of Italian mobile operator 3 Italia, and VimpelCom Ltd. ("VimpelCom"), parent company of WIND, entered into an agreement to form a 50/50 joint venture that will own and operate their telecommunications businesses in Italy.
- The joint venture holding company (Hutchison 3G Italy Investments S.à.r.l (the "JV Holdco")) will own 3 Italia and WIND, and each of CK Hutchison and VimpelCom will indirectly hold 50 percent of the shares in the joint venture.
- The Joint Venture won the European Union Commission approval for a merger creating Italy's largest wireless provider after they agreed to help a smaller rival, Iliad SA, become the country's fourth mobile carrier.

4.7.6 National Security in the Netherlands

In the Netherlands, any foreign investor seeking to acquire a direct or indirect qualifying holding[10] must seek a declaration of no objection from the Dutch Central Bank or the European Central Bank in the case of any bank institution. The regime covers any investment in a clearing institution, bank, UCITS manager, investment firm, entity for risk acceptance, premium pension institution or insurer which has its registered office in the Netherlands. The Dutch Central Bank has complete discretion in issuing such declaration. However, the grounds on which an application can be rejected are exhaustive.

4.7.6.1 Procedure

To complete its investigation, the Dutch central bank follows the following criteria:

- the completeness and correctness of the information provided by the applicant;
- the integrity of the prospective acquirer or of the persons who, by virtue of the prospective qualifying holding, will or will be able to determine or co-determine the policy of the financial undertaking;
- the financial soundness of the prospective acquirer, relative to the financial undertaking's business activities;
- the suitability of the persons who, by virtue of the prospective qualifying holding, will determine the day-to-day policy of the financial undertaking;
- the ability of the financial undertaking, as a result of the qualifying holding, to continue satisfying the prudential rules set pursuant to the Dutch Financial Supervision Act. Relevant considerations include whether the qualifying holding is structured such that supervision, information exchange and distribution of responsibilities between supervisory authorities are effective; and
- the existence of any good grounds for assuming that money laundering or terrorist financing play a role in the prospective acquisition or increase the risk of such activities being involved.

[10] More than 10% of the issued capital or voting rights.

4.8 Europe and the UK Case Study: BAE and Finmeccanica

In the European and UK context, there are no truly controversial deals to discuss. To a large extent, this is a credit to the way that the EU structure is effectively insulated from direct political meddling. The definition of national security for each Member State ends at its own border, with a broader concept of European security informal and relevant only to the extent that it impacts the individual Member State.

In joining the EU, each Member State knowingly gave up a significant measure of economic control within its own borders. No longer could it significantly restrict the flow of capital and labor among the European states. Along with that elevation of power to the European level went much of the power related to merger review.

While Member States have the power to raise a "public interest" exception, the Commission can override an abuse of that has power if the invocation is not compatible with the general principles and other provisions of Community law.

This is not to say that the UK has never invoked its right to raise a national security exception to a proposed merger. However, it has raised exceptions only in cases that fall squarely within the defense sector and even then, it has allowed transactions after negotiating remedies. A typical example is the 2002 joint venture that the UK's BAE Systems entered into with European Aeronautic Defense and Space Co. (Germany and France) and Finmeccanica (Italy). In the OFT report on the BAE Systems joint venture, the national security concerns are clearly separated out from competition concerns. Further, OFT states that it did not attempt to raise those concerns itself, rather they were raised by the Ministry of Defense ("MoD") and brought to OFT's attention. The Ministry of Defense was further responsible for negotiating a remedy to resolve its concerns with the parties.

The ultimate agreement negotiated by the MoD and endorsed by OFT contained several provisions to keep certain information and technology related to BAE's guided weapons business within the control of UK persons. OFT fully deferred to MoD, stating:

"OFT is not expert in national security matter and must, therefore, rely heavily on the representations made by the MoD." In many ways this decision is a model. It clearly separates out national security from competition. It allowed the deal to clear using a narrowly tailored, publicly available remedy agreement.

On the first impression, it is surprising that the European system, which combines national security review and competition review into a single process, seems to produce less drama than the US system, which endeavors to use wholly separate dual processes. However, this can be attributed to the working definition of national security in Europe and the unique structure of the EU. In terms of definition, the broadly phrased "public interest" could easily be expanded in practice, and perhaps will be in the future. But for the time being, the UK seems to have kept it focused within the traditional scope of national defense. Compared with a broad definition encompassing key infrastructure and economically crucial industries, there is relatively little gray area to define the limits of defense. Further, the companies operating in the defense industry are used to working closely with governments as major clients and are accustom to navigating export-controlled areas, and the boundaries between sensitive government-proprietary technology and that which can be sold to the public. These factors make for a smoother process unlikely to result in the politicization and diplomatic unpleasantness that has resulted from merger reviews in the United States and China. However, the other major factor that makes the European systems successful is attributable to the unique structure of the EU. As discussed above, the unusual confederation of European states means that attempts to expand the definition of national security can be overridden, or at least overshadowed, by having the primary review conducted by DG-Comp at the European level. While this system seems to work well, unfortunately it is not replicable for the United States or China, which operate as single nations.

CHAPTER 5

M&A Policies Review Under the Competition and National Security Laws in China

5.1 General

The legislative history of the AML can be traced back to 1987 when the State Council set up a legislative committee tasked with implementing antitrust legislation. Previous texts are:

(i) The Regulation on the Administration of Advertisement of the People's Republic of China, which stated that monopolies and unfair competition in advertising activities are prohibited.
(ii) The Anti-unfair Competition Law, which prohibited tied selling, price fixing, and bid rigging.
(iii) The Regulations for Merger and Acquisition of Domestic Enterprises by Foreign Investors, which granted both that if MOFCOM and SAIC the right to hear cases of overconcentration within any given industry.

The AML, which by many aspects, mirrors the EU Competition Laws, specifically Articles 101 and 102 of the EU Treaty, which prohibits abuse of dominant market positions and monopoly agreements. Its regulations require premerger notification based on the parties' total sales in China.[1]

[1] Susan Beth Farmer (2010): The Impact of China's Antitrust Law and Other Competition Policies on US Companies, *Loyola Consumer Law Review*, Vol. 23, No. 1, p. 36.

F. I. Lessambo, *Mergers in the Global Markets*,
https://doi.org/10.1007/978-3-030-43558-5_5

The 2008 law is enacted for the purpose of preventing and restraining monopolistic conducts, protecting fair market competition, enhancing economic efficiency, safeguarding the interests of consumers and the interests of the society as a whole, and promoting the healthy development of socialist market economy.[2] The AML prohibits "monopolistic conduct" divided as follows:

(1) monopoly agreements reached between undertakings;
(2) abuse of dominant market position by undertakings; and
(3) concentration of undertakings that lead, or may lead to elimination or restriction of competition.

Prior to 2018, two separate agencies were in charge of corporate abuse of dominance: (i) the National Development and Reform Commission (NDRC) and (ii) the State Administration for Industry and Commerce (SAIC), respectively. The NDRC was responsible for price-related abusive behavior, while the SAIC was in charge of non-price-related abusive behavior.[3] After March 2018, the two abovementioned authorities were combined into the Anti-Monopoly Bureau of State Administration of Market Regulation of China (AMB). Thus, the AMB is the single authority against monopolistic activities, regardless of whether the behavior is price-related. The enforcement authorities also were restructured in 2018. Three former Chinese antitrust enforcers, the NDRC, the SAIC, and the Anti-Monopoly Bureau of Ministry of Commerce, have been integrated into a single authority, the SAMR.[4]

5.2 Anti-competitive Monopoly

AML Article 13 defines monopoly agreement as any agreement, decision, or other concerted behavior that eliminates or restricts competition. The following agreements are automatically presumed to be illegal[5]:

[2] AML, Article 1.

[3] The other authority being the Anti-Monopoly Bureau of the Ministry of Commerce, which is responsible for merger control.

[4] Zhang Mao (2018): Devoted to Promoting Innovation and Reform in Market Regulation, available at http://samr.saic.gov.cn/xw/yw/zj/201805/t20180502_274005.html.

[5] AML, Articles 13 and 14.

(1) agreements on fixing or changing commodity prices;
(2) agreements on restricting the amount of commodities manufactured or marketed;
(3) agreements on splitting the sales market or the purchasing market for raw and semi-finished materials;
(4) agreements on restricting the purchase of new technologies or equipment, or the development of new technologies or products;
(5) agreements on joint boycotting of transactions; and
(6) other monopoly agreements confirmed as such by the authority for enforcement of the Anti-Monopoly Law under the State Council.
(7) on fixing the prices of commodities resold to a third party; and
(8) on restricting the lowest prices for commodities resold to a third party.

5.2.1 *Exemption to Prohibitions*

AML, Article 15 exempt the following agreements between undertakings when proved to be concluded for one of the following purposes:

(1) improving technologies, or engaging in research and development of new products; or
(2) improving product quality, reducing cost, and enhancing efficiency, unifying specifications and standards of products, or implementing specialized division of production;
(3) increasing the efficiency and competitiveness of small and medium-sized undertakings;
(4) serving public interests in energy conservation, environmental protection, and disaster relief;
(5) mitigating sharp decrease in sales volumes or obvious overproduction caused by economic depression;
(6) safeguarding legitimate interests in foreign trade and in economic cooperation with foreign counterparts; or
(7) other purposes as prescribed by law or the State Council.

5.3 Abuse of Dominant Position

AML Article 17 defines dominant market position means a market position held by undertakings that are capable of controlling the prices or quantities of commodities or other transaction terms in a relevant market, or preventing or exerting an influence on the access of other undertakings to the market. Undertakings holding dominant market positions are prohibited from doing the following by abusing their dominant market positions:

(1) selling commodities at unfairly high prices or buying commodities at unfairly low prices;
(2) without justifiable reasons, selling commodities at prices below cost;
(3) without justifiable reasons, refusing to enter into transactions with their trading counterparts;
(4) without justifiable reasons, allowing their trading counterparts to make transactions exclusively with themselves or with the undertakings designated by them;
(5) without justifiable reasons, conducting tie-in sale of commodities or adding other unreasonable trading conditions to transactions;
(6) without justifiable reasons, applying differential prices and other transaction terms among their trading counterparts who are on an equal footing; or
(7) other acts of abuse of dominant market positions confirmed as such by the authority for enforcement of the Anti-Monopoly Law under the State Council.

The dominant market position of an undertaking is determined based on the following factors[6]:

(1) its share on a relevant market and the competitiveness on the market;
(2) its ability to control the sales market or the purchasing market for raw and semi-finished materials;
(3) its financial strength and technical conditions;

[6] AML, Article 18.

(4) the extent to which other business mangers depend on it in transactions;
(5) the difficulty that other undertakings find in entering a relevant market; and
(6) other factors related to the determination of the dominant market position held by an undertaking.

Further, the conclusion that an undertaking holds a dominant market position may be deduced from any one of the following circumstances:

(1) the market shares of one undertaking accounts for half of the total in a relevant market;
(2) the joint market shares of two undertakings accounts for two-thirds of the total, in a relevant market; or
(3) the joint market shares of three undertakings accounts for three-fourths of the total in a relevant market.

However, if the market shares of one of the undertakings is less than one-tenths of the total, the undertaking is not considered to have a dominant market position. Likewise, an undertaking will not be considered to hold a dominant market position, if it possesses evidence establishing the facts that it does not hold a dominant position.

5.3.1 *The Chlorpheniramine API Case*[7]

On December 30, 2018, China's State Administration for Market Regulation (SAMR) issued an infringement decision imposing a total fine of RMB10.04 million (or US$1.46 million) on Hunan Er-Kang Medical Operation and Henan Jiushi Pharmaceutical for abusing their dominance in the supply of chlorpheniramine active pharmaceutical ingredients (API) in China. The two pharmaceutical companies, Hunan Er-kang and Henan Jiushi, were fined because they abused their dominance to charge excessive prices. SAMR reached out its conclusion by determining: (i) the relevant market, (ii) the dominance, (iii) the abusive practices.

[7] China's State Administration for Market Regulation (SAMR), December 30, 2018, http://samr.saic.gov.cn/gg/201901/t20190118_280436.html.

- Relevant market

Defining the relevant market is the fundamental prerequisite for identifying market dominance. According to the provisions of Paragraph 2 of Article 12 of Anti-Monopoly Law, the definition of the relevant market in the sense of anti-monopoly law is determined by the "range of goods" and "geographical scope" where a commodity or service needs to compete with others. In this case, the SAMR found:

- From a supply-sided perspective, domestic producers of chlorpheniramine API are required to obtain manufacturing and other approvals, while foreign suppliers are required to have the necessary approvals before being allowed to import chlorpheniramine API into China. Further, the facilities for manufacturing chlorpheniramine API cannot be used to produce other APIs.
- Accordingly, the SAMR found that there was limited demand and supply-sided substitutability for chlorpheniramine API, and concluded that chlorpheniramine API formed its own distinct product market.

- Dominance

- According to Paragraph 2 of Article 17 of the Anti-Monopoly Law, dominant market position refers to the undertaking(s) having the ability to control the price, quantity, or other trading conditions of products in a relevant market, or to hinder or affect other undertakings to enter the relevant market.
- According to Article 18 of the Anti-Monopoly Law, the following factors will be taken into consideration in calculating dominant market position: market share in relevant market, and the competition situation of the relevant market; ability to control the sales markets or the raw material purchasing markets; financial status and technical conditions of the undertaking; the degree of dependence of other undertakings; entry to relevant market by other undertakings; and other factors related to find a dominant market position.
- Such a determination is not always easy. Therefore, Article 19 of the Anti-Monopoly Law provides a per se rule, which states that undertakings meeting any of the following criteria can be assumed

to have a dominant market position: the relevant market share of one undertaking accounts for one-half or above; the joint relevant market share of two undertakings account for two-thirds or above; or the joint relevant market share of three undertakings account for three-quarters or above.[8]

- SAMR found that in 2017, the total market shares of the parties accounted for 96.38 per cent of China's chlorpheniramine API; and from January to July 2018, the combined market share was 88.55 per cent, and the market share of each of the parties exceeded 1:10.
- According to Article 19 of the AML, Hunan Er-kang and Henan Jiushi were presumed to be market dominators in the market of chlorpheniramine APIs in China. In assessing market dominance, the SAMR also considered the following factors: (i) the market for chlorpheniramine API was highly concentrated with only three active suppliers; (ii) Barriers to entry were high given the strict regulatory requirements and the need for drug manufacturers to obtain fresh approval for their drugs if they switched to other APIs.

- Abuse practices

  ■ Unfair pricing

- The two pharmaceutical companies abused their market dominance by refusing to deal with downstream drug manufacturers and tying chlorpheniramine APIs, Hunan Er-kang's starch capsules, and medicinal sucrose. Also the SAMR found that the two pharmaceutical companies abused their market dominance in the Chinese market for chlorpheniramine APIs by refusal to deal, and tying and causing anticompetitive impact on the relevant market.
- In so doing, Hunan Er-Kang was found to have violated Article 17(1) of the AML which prohibited selling goods at unfairly high prices, because while Hunan Er-Kang did not face any major changes to drug production and procurement costs, it sold chlorpheniramine API in July 2018 at a price of CNY 2940/kg, which was three to four times of the average cost to procure the same. Downstream

[8] You Minjian (2010): To Understand Abuse of Market Dominance in Anti-Monopoly Law, Chinaipmagazine.com.

drug manufacturers had to accept these prices as there were no alternatives and the parties controlled prices in the market.

■ Refusal to supply

- Hunan Er-Kang Medical Operation and Henan Jiushi Pharmaceutical have refused to supply chlorpheniramine API to downstream drug manufacturers on the false pretence of stock shortage.
- Alternatively, they had required drug manufacturers to pay excessive deposit amounts, increase the prices of the final drug products, and make commission payments. The situation was such that the downstream drug suppliers had no way of accepting these additional conditions, and held that the imposition of these conditions constituted a refusal to supply chlorpheniramine API. By their conduct, the parties have tightened the supply of chlorpheniramine API in the market and raised prices, resulting in some downstream drug manufacturers having to cut production as they were unable to purchase chlorpheniramine API.
- *Therefore*, Hunan Er-Kang Medical Operation and Henan Jiushi Pharmaceutical restricted competition in the market, and was in breach of Article 17(3) of the AML, which prohibits a dominant business operator from refusing to trade without a justified reason.

■ Abuse—Tying

- Hunan Er-Kang Medical Operation and Henan Jiushi Pharmaceutical were also found to have engaged in abusive tying by requiring downstream purchasers of chlorpheniramine API to also purchase starch capsules, medicinal cane sugar, and other medical supplements. The use of these medical supplements had no direct relation with the use of chlorpheniramine API, and purchasers typically bought them separately depending on their needs.
- Hunan Er-Kang Medical Operation and Henan Jiushi Pharmaceutical tying conduct restricted purchasers' choices in the market, and also allowed the parties to extend their dominance in the chlorpheniramine API to the market for such medicinal supplements.

- Hunan Er-Kang Medical Operation and Henan Jiushi Pharmaceutical therefore breached Article 17(5) of the AML for imposing tying requirements without objective reasons.

5.3.2 *The Qualcomm Case*

- In November 2013, the NDRC launched an investigation against Qualcomm for abusive dominance in several markets, including the licensing of SEPs for the CDMA, WCDMA, and LTE wireless communication standards, as well as the supply of baseband chips.
- Qualcomm was accused of abusing its dominant position by charging excessive royalty fees to Chinese companies as well as for bundling and requiring licensees to cross-license their patents for fee.
- On February 10, 2015, NDRC announced that it had concluded its investigation by ordering Qualcomm to cease certain abuses of market dominance and to pay a fine of RMB 6.088B (approximately $930M USD). NDRC found Qualcomm to have violated the AML in several markets in which it has a dominant position (the SEP licensing market for CDMA, WCDMA, and LTE baseband chips, in which NDRC found Qualcomm to have a 100% share, and the baseband chip markets themselves, in which it found Qualcomm to have 93%, 54%, and 96% shares, respectively).
- NDRC's decision highlighted three areas of allegedly anticompetitive conduct:
    - Charging unfairly high patent royalties. NDRC found that Qualcomm had artificially inflated royalties charged to wireless SEP licensees in two ways: one, by charging royalties on expired patents, and two, by demanding free cross-licenses for patents from SEP licensees. Qualcomm had failed to disclose to its licensees the patents for which it had charged its licensees royalties, NDRC concluded, thus depriving licensees of the opportunity to negotiate for access on fair terms. In addition, NDRC found that Qualcomm's practices of bundling SEPs and non-SEPs and charging licensees at rates based on the net selling prices of handset devices was unfair and led to excessive royalties.

      NDRC's finding is particularly striking given the public criticism of potential liability for excessive royalties raised by

Western officials before NDRC had concluded its inquiry. For example, Federal Trade Commission Chairwoman Edith Ramirez criticized NDRC for taking such an approach. "I am seriously concerned by these reports [indicating that China's antitrust authorities may be willing to impose liability based solely on the royalty terms that a patent owner demands]," she stated, because they "suggest an enforcement policy focused on reducing royalty payments for local implementers as a matter of industrial policy, rather than protecting competition and long- run consumer welfare." The Assistant Attorney General for Antitrust at the US Department of Justice, William Baer, also announced that he shared the Chairwoman's concerns and added: "Using antitrust enforcement to reduce the price firms pay to license technology owned and developed by others is short sighted. Any short-term gains derived from imposing what are effectively price controls will diminish incentives of existing and potential licensors to compete and innovate over the long-term, depriving jurisdictions of the benefits of an innovation based- economy." Jack Lew, the Secretary of the US Department of the Treasury, is reported to have sent a letter to his Chinese counterpart that, The Wall Street Journal reported, warned China that its investigations into non-Chinese companies could "devalue foreign intellectual property" and "have serious implications for relations" between the United States and China.

- Tying sales of non-SEP licenses without justifiable cause. NDRC also found that Qualcomm tied licenses of non-SEPs to licenses of SEPs, conditioning licenses of SEPs on non-essential non-SEPs. NDRC found that this conduct harmed licensees, which were limited in their ability to choose from alternative non-SEPs or "design around" Qualcomm's non-SEPs.
- Imposing unreasonable terms on the sale of baseband chips. According to the NDRC, Qualcomm had conditioned certain sales of baseband chips upon "non-challenge provisions" whereby its purchasers had to agree not to challenge the validity of Qualcomm's patents as a condition to receiving the baseband chips.

Qualcomm accepted NDRC's decision and also adopted a "rectification plan," which included commitments to conform company policies to the constraints provided by NDRC.

5.3.3 *The Mercedes-Benz and Dongfeng Nissan Case*

- In 2015, two regional regulators under the administration of NDRC levied fines against Mercedes-Benz and Dongfeng Nissan (Nissan's China joint venture with Dongfeng Motor), as well as their respective dealers, for resale price maintenance in violation of the AML. Specifically, the regulators concluded that the manufacturers and their dealers had reached and implemented certain agreements to fix minimum resale prices, thereby excluding and restricting market competition. Mercedes-Benz and Dongfeng Nissan were therefore fined RMB 350M ($53M USD) and RMB 123M ($19M USD), respectively. The dealers were also subject to fines varying from 1 to 4% of their turnover for the previous year.

5.4 Concentration of Undertakings

AML, Article 20 defines "concentration undertaking" as:

(1) merger of undertakings;
(2) control over other undertakings gained by an undertaking through acquiring their shares or assets; and
(3) control over other undertakings or the ability capable of exerting a decisive influence on the same gained by an undertaking through signing contracts or other means.

Whenever an intended concentration reaches the threshold level set up by the State Council, the parties must declare in advance to the authority for enforcement of the Anti-Monopoly Law under the State Council.[9] However, certain concentration undertakings are dispensed from the prior

[9] AML, Article 21.

declaration to the authority for enforcement of the Anti-monopoly Law under the State Council if[10]:

(1) one of the undertakings involved in the concentration owns 50 percent or more of the voting shares or assets of each of the other undertakings; or
(2) one and the same undertaking not involved in the concentration owns 50 percent or more of the voting shares or assets of each of the undertakings involved in the concentration.

Whenever a prior declaration is mandated, the parties must submit, in written, the following documents and materials:

(1) declaration in writing;
(2) explanation of the impact to be exerted by the concentration on competition in a relevant market;
(3) concentration agreement;
(4) the financial report of each of the undertakings in the previous fiscal year, which is audited by a certified public accountant firm; and
(5) other documents and materials as specified by the authority for enforcement of the Anti-Monopoly Law under the State Council.

The following factors[11] shall be taken into consideration in the review of concentration of undertakings:

(1) the market shares of the undertakings involved in concentration in a relevant market and their power of control over the market;
(2) the degree of concentration in relevant market;
(3) the impact of their concentration on assess to the market and technological advance;
(4) the impact of their concentration on consumers and the other relevant undertakings concerned;
(5) the impact of their concentration on the development of the national economy; and

[10] AML, Article 22.

[11] AML, Article 27.

(6) other factors which the authority for enforcement of the Anti-Monopoly Law under the State Council deems to need consideration in terms of its impact on market competition.

Where the authority for enforcement of the Anti-Monopoly Law under the State Council does not prohibit the concentration of undertakings, it may decide to impose additional, restrictive conditions for lessening the negative impact exerted by such concentration on competition.[12]

5.5 Abuse of Administrative Power to Eliminate or Restrict Competition

Administrative departments and other organizations authorized by laws or regulations to perform the function of administering public affairs may not abuse their administrative power to require, or require in disguised form, units or individuals to deal in, purchase or use only the commodities supplied by the undertakings, nor impede the free flow of commodities between different regions, nor exclude non-local undertakings from participating, or restrict their participation.

5.6 Investigation into Suspected Monopolistic Conducts

The authority for enforcement of the Anti-Monopoly Law must investigate any suspected monopolistic conduct according to law. When conducting investigations into a suspected monopolistic conduct, the authority for enforcement of the Anti-Monopoly Law may take the following measures:

(1) conducting inspection of the business places or the relevant premises of the undertakings under investigation;
(2) making inquiries of the undertakings under investigation, the interested parties, or other units or individuals involved, and requesting them to provide relevant explanations;
(3) consulting and duplicating the relevant documents and materials of the undertakings under investigation, the interested parties and

[12] AML, Article 29.

other relevant units and individuals, such as bills, certificates, agreements, account books, business correspondence, and electronic data;

(4) sealing up or seizing relevant evidence; and
(5) inquiring about the bank accounts of the undertakings under investigation.

The authority for enforcement of the Anti-Monopoly Law and its staff members are obligated to keep confidential any commercial secrets that come to their knowledge during the conduct of the investigation; and the interested parties or other relevant units or individuals must cooperate with the authority for enforcement of the Anti-Monopoly Law in performing their duties. Where after investigation into and verification of the suspected monopolistic conduct, the authority for enforcement of the Anti-Monopoly Law concludes that it constitutes a monopolistic conduct, the said authority shall make a decision on how to deal with it in accordance with law and may make the matter known to the public.[13] The authority for enforcement of the Anti-Monopoly Law may decide to suspend the investigation. In the decision must clearly be stated the details of the undertakings' commitments.[14]

Where the authority for enforcement of the Anti-Monopoly Law decides to suspend investigation, it must oversee the fulfillment of the commitments made by the undertaking. Where the undertaking fulfills its commitments, the authority for enforcement of the Anti-Monopoly Law may decide to terminate the investigation.

In any of the following circumstances, the authority for enforcement of the Anti-Monopoly Law shall resume investigation:

(1) The undertakings concerned fail to fulfill its commitments;
(2) Material changes have taken place in respect of the facts on which the decision to suspend investigation was based; or
(3) The decision to suspend investigation was based on incomplete or untrue information provided by the undertaking concerned.

[13] AML, Article 44.

[14] AML, Article 45.

5.7 The Simplified Procedure

On February 11, 2014, MOFCOM announced its simplified procedure for "simple cases" that do not raise competition concerns in the PRC. The new procedure aims to speed up the merger review process which could see "60 per cent of notified transactions" cleared within Phase 1. The simplified procedure has two key advantages[15]: (i) it significantly shortens the time taken to obtain merger approvals and (ii) reduces the administrative burden on notifying parties for simple cases. The simplified procedure does not apply to all transactions. It is only available for the following types of transactions[16]:

- offshore joint ventures with no activities in the PRC;
- changes from joint to sole control of a joint venture (except where the sole parent and the joint venture compete in the same market); or
- transaction where the parties have a combined market share of less than 15 per cent if they compete in the same market; and each have market share of less than 25 per cent if they are active in any vertically related or neighboring markets.

5.8 Notification Threshold

Notification generally is required under the AML if (1) the total worldwide turnover of all parties in the previous fiscal year exceeds RMB 10 billion (approximately $1.5 billion), and the PRC turnover of at least 2 parties exceeds RMB 400 million (approximately $62 million), or (2) the total PRC turnover of all parties in the previous fiscal year exceeds RMB 2 billion (approximately $314 million) and the PRC turnover of at least 2 of the parties exceeds RMB 400 million. State Council Rule on the Notification Thresholds for Concentration of Undertakings, Decree No. 529 (August 3, 2008).

[15] Slaughter and May (2016): Competition Law in China, p. 16.

[16] Article 2, Simplified Procedure Notice.

5.9 Gun-Jumping/Failure to Notify

In 2012, MOFCOM published the Interim Measures on Investigation of Failure to Notify Concentrations of Undertakings. MOFCOM has now published 17 penalty decisions since 2014, eight of which involved the formation of joint ventures and nine concerned share acquisitions (two of which were acquisitions of minority stakes). More recently, MOFCOM penalized companies for gun-jumping in "multi-step" transactions (Canon/Toshiba and Meinian Onehealth/Ciming Health). MOFCOM may impose a penalty of up to a maximum of RMB 500,000 and the penalties to date have ranged from RMB 150,000 to RMB 400,000. The director general of the Anti-Monopoly Bureau in MOFCOM had previously warned that a failure to notify could lead to the transaction being unwound if it is a case, which raises competition concerns. Further, there have been reports that there are proposals to introduce amendments to the AML to increase fines for failure to notify and other possible punitive measures.

5.10 Legal Liabilities

5.10.1 General Liabilities

China's AML has provided the following liabilities:

- Where an undertaking, in violation of the provisions of the AML, concludes and implements a monopoly agreement, the authority for enforcement of the Anti-Monopoly Law must instruct it to discontinue the violation, confiscate its unlawful gains, and, in addition, impose on it a fine of not less than one percent but not more than 10 percent of its sales achieved in the previous year. If such monopoly agreement has not been implemented, it may be fined not more than RMB 500,000 yuan.[17]
- If the business manage, on its own initiative, reports to the authority for enforcement of the Anti-Monopoly Law about the monopoly agreement reached, and provides material evidence, the AML authority may, at its discretion, mitigate, or exempt the undertaking from punishment.

[17] AML, Article 46.

- Where a trade association, in violation of the provisions of this Law, has arranged the undertaking in the trade to reach a monopoly agreement, the authority for enforcement of the Anti-Monopoly Law may impose on it a fine of not more than 500,000 yuan. If the circumstances are serious, the administrative department for the registration of public organizations may cancel the registration of the trade association in accordance with law.
- Where an undertaking, in violation of the provisions of the AML, abuses its dominant market position, the authority for enforcement of the Anti-Monopoly Law must instruct it to discontinue such violation, confiscate its unlawful gains, and, in addition, impose on it a fine of not less than one percent but not more than 10 percent of its sales achieved in the previous year.[18]
- Where the undertakings, in violation of the provisions of the AML, implement concentration, the authority for enforcement of the Anti-Monopoly Law under the State Council must instruct them to discontinue such concentration, and within a specified time limit to dispose of their shares or assets, transfer the business, and adopt other necessary measures to return to the state prior to the concentration, and it may impose on them a fine of not more than 500,000 yuan.[19]

To determine the specific amount of fines prescribed in Articles 46, 47, and 48, the authority for enforcement of the Anti-Monopoly Law must consider such factors as the nature, extent, and duration of the violations.

- Where the monopolistic conduct of an undertaking has caused losses to another person, it shall bear civil liabilities according to law.[20]
- Where an administrative development or an organization authorized by laws or regulations to perform the function of administering public affairs abuses its administrative power to eliminate or restrict competition, the department at a higher level shall instruct it to rectify; the leading person directly in charge and the other persons directly responsible shall be given administrative sanctions in accordance with

[18] AML, Article 47.

[19] AML, Article 48.

[20] AML, Article 50.

law. The authority for enforcement of the Anti-Monopoly Law may submit a proposal to the relevant department at a higher level for handling the matter according to law.

- Where otherwise provided for by laws or administrative regulations in respect of administrative departments or organizations authorized by laws or regulations to perform the function of administering public affairs that abuse their administrative power to eliminate or restrict competition, such provisions shall prevail.[21]
- Where, during the review and investigation conducted by the authority for enforcement of the Anti-Monopoly Law, a unit or individual refuses to provide relevant materials or information, or provides false materials or information, or conceals, or destroys, or transfers evidence, or refuses to submit to or obstructs investigation in any other manner, the authority for enforcement of the Anti-Monopoly Law shall instruct it/him to rectify, and a fine of not more than 20,000 yuan shall be imposed on the individual and not more than 200,000 yuan on the unit; if the circumstances are serious, a fine of not less than 20,000 yuan but not more than 100,000 yuan shall be imposed on the individual and not less than 200,000 yuan but not more than one million yuan on the unit, and if a crime is constituted, criminal liability shall be investigated for in accordance with law.[22]
- Where an undertaking is dissatisfied with the decision made by the authority for enforcement of the Anti-Monopoly Law in accordance with the provisions of Article 28 or 29 of this Law, it may first apply for administrative reconsideration according to law; and if it is dissatisfied with the decision made after administrative reconsideration, it may bring an administrative action before the court according to law.
- Where an undertaking is dissatisfied with any decision made by the authority for enforcement of the Anti-Monopoly Law other than the decisions specified in the preceding paragraph, it may apply for administrative reconsideration or bring an administrative action before the court according to law.
- Where a staff member of the authority for enforcement of the Anti-Monopoly Law abuses his power, neglects his duty, engages

[21] AML, Article 51.

[22] AML, Article 52.

in malpractices for personal gain, or divulges commercial secrets he comes to have access to in the course of law enforcement, which constitutes a crime, he shall be investigated for criminal liability according to law; and if his case is not serious enough to constitute a crime, he shall be given an administrative sanction according to law.

5.10.2 Specific Remedies

- The Fair, Reasonable, And Non-Discriminatory (FRAND) commitment

A FRAND commitment is a voluntary agreement between the standard-setting organization and the holder of standard-essential patents. Courts in the United States, the EU, as well as in other jurisdictions, and competition enforcement agencies, have found that, in appropriate circumstances, the implementer of a standard is an intended third-party beneficiary of the FRAND agreement, and, as such, is entitled to certain rights conferred by that agreement. A FRAND commitment is meant to limit a patent holder to a reasonable royalty on the economic value of its patented technology itself, apart from the value associated with incorporation of the patented technology into the standard. The FRAND requirement facilitates widespread use of the standard and insures that each standard-essential patent (SEP) owner benefits from use of the patent without gaining an unfair bargaining advantage.[23] In Nokia/Alcatel-Lucent, MOFCOM concluded that the acquisition would strengthen Nokia's position in the communications technology SEP market and increase the concentration on that specific market.[24]

- Continued R&D

MOFCOM/SAMR often alleges these specific remedies as a means of addressing concerns regarding loss of innovation, structural remedies, or behavior remedies (or a combination of both). For instance, in

[23] Jeffrey I.D. Lewis (2014): What Is "FRAND" All About? The Licensing of Patents Essential to an Accepted Standard, *Cardozo Law Review*.

[24] Cheng Liu, Audrey Yumeng Li, and Jeff Liu (2019): Navigating Through Merger Control Review in China—Challenges for U.S. Companies During a Time of Uncertainty, https://www.competitionpolicyinternational.com.

UTC/Rockwell Collins, SAMR required all of UTC's research projects on oxygen systems, including all assets, IP, R&D contracts, and employees participating in the research projects to be divested. Moreover, parties were requested by MOFCOM/SAMR to commit to continued R&D investment promoting certain levels of innovation benefiting the aviation industry and aircraft platforms in China.[25]

- Chinese stakeholders' complaints

Whenever MOFCOM determined that the relevant market(s) for the challenged product(s) is global, it may impose specific remedies to alleviate the grievance. For instance, in Bayer/Monsanto, MOFCOM required that the parties allowed to all relevant Chinese App developers access to the their digital platform on FRAND terms within five years after the parties' digital agricultural platform comes into China.[26]

5.11 M&A Review Under the National Security Laws in China

China maintains a decentralized review process split between central and local government authorities and retains the power to restrict or block any foreign investment that may have a significant impact on national economic security. Like the United States, the Chinese Government has not defined key terms in the 2006 regulations, contributing to a lack of transparency in the review process.

5.11.1 *National Security Concept in China*

In 2006, China began to adopt laws and regulations to describe the procedures it uses to review, and potentially block, proposed foreign acquisitions that it deems are not in China's national interest. According to Chinese officials, two regulations provide the primary framework for China's foreign investment review. First, the 2006 Provisions for Merger

[25] Cheng Liu, Audrey Yumeng Li, and Jeff Liu (2019): Navigating Through Merger Control Review in China—Challenges for U.S. Companies During a Time of Uncertainty, https://www.competitionpolicyinternational.com.

[26] Idem.

and Acquisition of Domestic Enterprises by Foreign Investors (the 2006 regulations) are the most important rules for managing foreign investment. The 2006 regulations establish the need for government approval of foreign investment if the transaction (i) affects national economic security, (ii) involves a major industry, or (iii) results in the transfer of famous trademarks or traditional Chinese brands.[27]

If foreign investors fail to apply for approval, the Chinese Government has the legal authority to force divestiture if a transaction causes or may cause significant impact on China's economic security.

Second, the Chinese Catalog for the Guidance of Foreign Investment Industries (the Catalog) restricts foreign investment in specified sectors. A revised version of the Catalog was issued by the NDRC in November 2007. It assigns industry sectors to one of the three categories: "encouraged," "restricted," and "prohibited." Investment in unlisted sectors is automatically considered "permitted." However, the Catalog does not prohibit investment for stated reasons, or define national security, although some industries clearly fall into that category, including weapons and ammunition manufacturing, mining and processing of radioactive materials and rare earth metals, and construction and operation of power networks. Other sectors are prohibited based on a broader definition of national security, including film, television, book publishing, and other media production.

Other Chinese laws, regulations, and opinions also regulate foreign investment. However, only the Anti-Monopoly Law does so explicitly for national security.

Article 31 of the AML provides that:

"Besides the examination on concentration in accordance with this Law, the examination on national security according to the relevant regulations of the State shall be conducted as well on the acquisition of domestic undertakings by foreign capital."

The AML does not define the concept of "national security," leaving it the Chinese enforcement agencies with a significant amount of discretion.

[27] Idem.

Several Chinese Government entities are involved in the review of foreign investment, including the following[28]:

- State Council: The State Council is China's chief executive and administrative authority. Members include the Premier, as the head of government; a variable number of vice premiers; 22 ministers; and State Council commission directors.
- National Development and Reform Commission (NDRC): The NDRC is the State Council's economic policy planning arm. According to United States and industry officials, it is a powerful macroeconomic management agency with broad planning control over the Chinese economy, and specific control over heavy industry. United States and industry officials have stated that the NDRC is deeply involved in the review of foreign investment transactions.
- Ministry of Commerce (MOFCOM): MOFCOM is under the State Council and is charged with managing China's external economic relations. Its duties include formulating trade policy, regulating foreign participation in markets, implementing import and export quotas, implementing trade and economic cooperation policies, and guiding foreign investment.
- State-owned Assets Supervision and Administration Commission (SASAC): SASAC is a commission under the State Council that represents the central government's ownership interests in 159 state-owned enterprises (SOE). As part of its duties, SASAC guides SOE reform, drafts laws and regulations on SOE management, and supervises the preservation of SOE value.
- State Administration for Industry and Commerce (SAIC): SAIC is a State Council ministry in charge of supervising market competition, investigating illegal trade, regulating contract performance, and handling trademark registration and administration.
- In addition to the above, industrial associations and competitors can trigger security review.[29]

[28] United States Government Accountability Office (July 2008): Foreign Investment: Laws and Policies Regulating Foreign Investment in 10 Countries, pp. 42–43.

[29] Vivienne Bath (2013): National Security and Chinese Investment Policy, *Harvard Business Law Review* (online), Vol. 3, p. 86.

5.11.2 The Review Process

Under the AML, MOFCOM's pre-concentration anti-monopoly review consists of a 30-day initial review plus a 90-day further review, with the possibility of a 60-day extended review under extreme circumstances. The review commences only after the notifying parties have submitted all required documents. MOFCOM can still require additional materials. MOFCOM comprehensively reviewed this business operator concentration from several aspects, including:

- Market shares in the relevant markets and the power of control over the markets of the business operators participating in the concentration

Article 12 of the AML defines the relevant market as the commodity scope or territorial scope within which the business operators compete against each other during a certain period of time for specific commodities or services.[30]

- The degree of market concentration of the relevant markets

Article 27(2) of AML requires that the degree of market concentration in the relevant market be taken into account in the examination of the concentration of business operators.[31]

- The effect on market entry
- The impact of the business operator concentration on market access and technological advancement
- The impact of the business operator concentration on consumers and other relevant business operators
- The effects on consumers and other businesses concerned
- The impact of the business operator concentration on the development of the national economy.

[30] Huang Xian Yu (2015): Huiyuan's Acquisition by Coca-Cola in PRC—Case Analysis, *Journal of Economics, Business and Management*, Vol. 3, No. 2, February 2015, p. 271.

[31] Huang Xian Yu (2015): Huiyuan's Acquisition by Coca-Cola in PRC—Case Analysis, *Journal of Economics, Business and Management*, Vol. 3, No. 2, February 2015, p. 272.

China has a nominal process for reviewing all foreign mergers and acquisitions. Factors affecting the review process include (1) competitor firms generating negative public attention that may influence relevant officials, (2) bureaucratic infighting, (3) differences in priorities between the local and central-level Chinese Government related to their motivations for the approval of foreign investment, (4) the Chinese political calendar, and (5) regulatory ambiguity and lack of procedural transparency.

All five factors can affect the outcome of a particular review, resulting in an application process that is unpredictable for investors. All transactions must go through the Ministry of Commerce[32]:

- Step 1: All foreign investors must apply to the local or provincial-level Ministry of Commerce when attempting to merge with or acquire a Chinese firm.
- Step 2: Most small transactions are reviewed and approved by the local-level Ministry of Commerce and then go to the local- or provincial-level government for registration and licensing.
- Step 3: The central-level Ministry of Commerce reviews large or politically sensitive transactions. Factors affecting political sensitivity might include the size of the transaction, whether a state-owned enterprise is involved, whether the sector itself is sensitive, and whether actors involved in the transaction are connected to the State Council.
- Step 4: Other relevant actors provide "preapproval." This step generally determines whether or not a transaction will be approved. The NDRC plays an important role in the review as the lead economic planning agency, as does SASAC in cases involving Chinese state-owned enterprises.
- Step 5: The central-level Ministry of Commerce reviews the application and provides the official approval or denial. If another governmental entity has jurisdiction, the Ministry of Commerce will rely on it to determine approval or denial. Within six months of a transaction being approved, the Ministry of Commerce issues a certificate of foreign investment.

[32] Idem, pp. 46–47.

- Step 6: Once the central-level Ministry of Commerce issues a certificate of foreign investment, the foreign company has 1 month to obtain a business license and register the business with the State Administration of Industry and Commerce.

Further, Article 19 of the AML gives a statutory definition of market dominance and indicates that a single business operator with more than a 50% market share will face a rebuttable presumption of dominance.

Article 27 of the AML enumerates several typical factors for MOFCOM to take into consideration in assessing the potential effects of a transaction under review. These factors include the market shares of the business operators, the degree of market concentration of the relevant markets, the impact of the concentration on market access and technological advancement and on consumers, and other relevant business operators.

5.11.3 Blocked Deals in China

Because China's situation is still developing and a national security review system has only recently established, two case studies are necessary to elaborate the conditions foreign investors and Chinese regulators face. The first case, Carlyle and Xugong, demonstrates the impact of national security on general approval of foreign acquisitions prior to the AML. The second and more central case for this paper's discussion, Coca-Cola and Huiyuan, supports the argument that AML enforcement has been politicized by national security concerns. Examining these cases is necessary to appreciate the breadth of national security's definition in China and also the ways that it can appear in somewhat unexpected places.

1. Carlyle Group and Xugong

- In October 2005, The Carlyle Group ("Carlyle") announced its intention to buy an 85% stake in Xugong Construction Machinery Group ("Xugong"). Xugong was the largest construction machinery maker in China and under the ownership of the Xuzhou local government.
- XCMC is currently owned by Xuzhou Construction Machinery Group (XCMG), which will retain a 15 percent holding in the company. XCMG is wholly owned by the city government of Xuzhou.

- The agreement followed a lengthy and rigorous auction process, with two rounds and six international bidders. The auction was conducted under the guidance of the Xuzhou Asset Exchange Centre in accordance with central and local government regulations on the transfer of state-owned assets, which emphasize open, equitable and impartial principles. JP Morgan was the independent financial advisor to XCMG and XCMC in the transaction. All relevant authorities were invited to participate in the thorough and detailed appraisal process for all bidders.
- Both sides praised the deal:

  "This is the right choice for a win-win outcome. It will unload our heavy historical burdens as an SOE, build an energetic and competitive system in the company, help us reach out to more international channels, and realize the dream of several generations of Xugong people to build an international brand. Carlyle will also bring technological innovation and new investment projects. XCMC will become a much stronger enterprise and be prepared for international expansion."[33]

  We are excited about this important investment in XCMC, one of our largest in China. The XCMC management team has built a solid business, and we look forward to working with them to create a leading international construction equipment company with deep roots in China's fast developing industrial sector and creating an international brand.[34]

- The transaction has obtained Xuzhou government approval, and is now in the process of completing Jiangsu provincial government approval and appropriate central government regulatory approvals.
- The deal immediately triggered widespread concerns over national economic security in China.
- In October 2006, Carlyle reduced its offer from the initial 85% stake to 50% equity and gave up the right to appoint the Chairman.

[33] The Chairman of XCMC, Mr. Wang Min., at www.carlyle.com/news-room-release-archive.

[34] Managing Director and Co-head of the Carlyle Asia Buyout Group, Mr. X.D. Yang, at www.carlyle.com/news-room-release-archive.

- Seeking to appease the political turmoil, Carlyle revised for the second time its proposal to 45% equity to be paid in two instalments—39% upfront and 9% at a later date.
- After three years of waiting and making additional concessions without securing MOFCOM approval, the deal was abandoned in July 2008.

2. Coca-Cola and Huiyuan Juice

The relevant facts under the case are as follow:

- on September 3, 2008, Coca-Cola, Atlantic Industries (a wholly-owned subsidiary of Coca-Cola), and Huiyuan jointly announced that ABN AMRO, a Dutch bank, would act on behalf of Atlantic Industries to make a conditional cash offer to acquire all of Huiyuan's issued shares and outstanding convertible bonds.
- Huiyuan is incorporated in the Cayman Islands and listed on the Hong Kong Stock Exchange.
- Coke had offered HK$12.20 a share in cash, almost treble that of Huiyuan's last closing price prior to the announcement of the deal.
- Huiyuan controlled 8.5% of China's fruit and vegetable juice market and 40% of its pure juice market; while Coke already controlled more than half of 40% of China's soft drink market and 12% of its fruit and vegetable juice market.
- To proceed with the transaction, Coca-Cola filed with MOFCOM to seek an anti-monopoly clearance.
- From Coca-Cola's perspective, buying Huiyuan was a chance to penetrate China's seductive fruit and vegetable juice segment, in keeping with its global strategy of diversifying beyond its traditional carbonated drinks stronghold. China's fruit and vegetable juice market grew at a tempting 15% rate last year to US$2 billion, even as global demand for carbonated drinks fell. Coke already claims over half of China's soft drink market, and around a 10% share in the fruit and vegetable juice market, but has yet to make inroads selling pure juice.
- On November 20, 2008, MOFCOM officially started the first stage review of the transaction and notified Coca-Cola accordingly. On December 20, 2008, MOFCOM decided to conduct a further

review, and on March 18, 2009, MOFCOM finished that review before the initial second stage 90 days' deadline of March 20, 2009.

- Opinions were solicited by means of written requests, forums, hearings, on-site investigation, and discussions with interested parties.
- In March 2009, MOFCOM's Anti-Monopoly Bureau announced a decision to prohibit the acquisition of China Huiyuan Juice Company by Coca-Cola. The decision was made under Article 28 of the AML, which is the appropriate article authorizing prohibition of concentrations which would restrict competition.
- MOFCOM statements offer three reasons why MOFCOM decided to prohibit the acquisition:

  (a) First is that Coca-Cola would be able to extend its dominant position in the carbonated beverages market into the market for fruit juice.

  "The concentration would have narrowed the room for the survival of medium and small-sized domestic juice firms, creating an unhealthy impact on the competitive structure of China's juice beverage market."

  (b) Second, the acquisition would concentrate two of China's most famous juice brands—Huiyuan and Minute Maid—under the control of a single powerful company.

  (c) Third, the concentration would make it harder for small and medium-sized juice companies to survive. Nowhere among the reasons does MOFCOM mention national economic security or the value of the Huiyuan brand to China's development goals.

PART III

Global Enforcement and Co-operation

CHAPTER 6

Extraterritorial Competence of the United States, the EU, and China Competition Laws

6.1 General

Term "extraterritoriality" refers to the exercise by a sovereign state of jurisdiction over foreigners in respect of acts done outside the borders of that state. In the context of competition policy, the issue of extraterritoriality would arise if the business practices of firm(s) in one country had an anticompetitive effect in another country which the latter considered to be in violation of its laws.

6.2 Extraterritorial Competence of the U.S. Competition Laws

At its inception, the application of U.S. antitrust law was thought to be limited to the territory of the United States.[1] However, things had changed. The extraterritorial reach of U.S. antitrust laws has for a long time been met with the approval of the U.S. courts. The two U.S. antitrust provisions that most frequently give rise to extraterritorial jurisdiction are Sections 1 and 2 of the Sherman Act. Section 1 declares illegal "every contract, combination … or conspiracy," in restraint of trade or commerce among the several states, or with foreign nations, while

[1] American Banana Co. v. United Fruit Co., 213 U.S. 347 (1909).

F. I. Lessambo, *Mergers in the Global Markets*,
https://doi.org/10.1007/978-3-030-43558-5_6

Section 2 makes it a felony for any person to "monopolize ... or combine or conspire..., to monopolize any part of the trade or commerce among the several states, or with foreign nations."[2]

Section 6a of the Act of the Sherman Act provides, under specific conditions, an exemption with respect to foreign nations as follows:

Sections 1–7 of this title shall not apply to conduct involving trade or commerce (other than import trade or import commerce) with foreign nations unless:

1. such conduct has a direct, substantial, and reasonably foreseeable effect
   (a) on trade or commerce which is not trade or commerce with foreign nations, or on import trade or import commerce with foreign nations; or
   (b) on export trade or export commerce with foreign nations, of a person engaged in such trade or commerce in the United States; and
2. such effect gives rise to a claim under the provisions of Sections 1–7 of this title, other than this section.

The legislative history of the FTAIA states the Act:

> Is intended neither to prevent nor to encourage additional judicial recognition of the special international characteristics of transactions. If a court determines that the requirements for subject matter jurisdiction are met, this bill would have no effect on the courts' ability to employ notions of comity,[3] or otherwise to take account of the international character of the transaction.

Thus, the Sherman Act extends its application to all international business arrangements where the effects of such agreement are felt in the

[2] Roger P. Alford (1992): The Extraterritorial Application of Antitrust Laws: The United States and European Community Approaches, *Virginia Journal of International Law*, pp. 6–7.

[3] Timberlane Lumber Co. vs. Bank of America, 549 F.2d 1287 (3rd Cir. 1979).

United States. In the Alcoa case, the Second Circuit held that the Sherman Act also applies to acts outside United States territory if such acts were intended to affect imports and did affect them.[4]

Likewise, the Clayton Act, which regulates mergers and acquisitions recognized U.S. jurisdiction to U.S. agencies and courts whenever an international merger has some direct, substantial, and reasonably foreseeable effects in the United States.

6.2.1 The Assertion of U.S. Extraterritorial Effects Over Time

The external outreach of both the Sherman Act and the Clayton Act took quite some time to become part of the U.S. doctrine. For the very first time, the question of extraterritorial application of the Sherman Act was submitted to the U.S. Supreme Court in the American Banana case. The American Banana Company alleged that the United Fruit Company had restrained trade in bananas in violation of the Sherman Act by unlawfully seizing one of its plantations in Panama with the help of Costa Rican authorities. All the acts complained of were committed outside the territory of the United States, including the defendant's alleged inducements of the Costa Rican government to monopolize the banana trade. The highest court rejected such a notion, holding that "a construction of any statute as intended to be confined in its operation and effect to the territorial limits over which the lawmaker has general and legitimate power."[5] The Alcoa case was somehow particular, the Second Circuit was the court of last resort because the Supreme Court did not have enough justices who could hear the case.

More than three decades later, the United States stance would chance through the activism of the Second Circuit in the Alcoa case. The Circuit departed from the U.S. Supreme Court territoriality principle to extend the reach of the Sherman Act to agreements conducted outside the United States if they were intended to affect imports and did affect them. The Second Circuit moved on to hold:

[4] United States v. Aluminium Co. of America, 148 F.2d 416, 444 (2nd Cir. 1945).

[5] Am. Banana v. United Fruit Co., 213 U.S. 347 (1909).

> courts should not … read general words, such as those in the Sherman Act, without regard to the limitations customarily observed by nations upon the exercise of their powers; limitations which generally correspond to those fixed by the Conflicts of Laws.

Later on, the U.S. Supreme Court would surrender to the Second Circuit doctrine to accept the extraterritorial application of both the Sherman and the Clayton Acts. A nuance will be added in the Hartford Fire Insurance Company where the Supreme Court was again petitioned to look inside the alleged anticompetitive conduct under the U.S. Sherman Act. In Hartford, nineteen states and a number of private parties filed suit under the Sherman Act against four domestic primary insurers and various reinsurers, including certain London reinsurers, alleging that the defendants had conspired to make certain kinds of environmental insurance coverage unavailable in the United States. The plaintiffs alleged that the defendants had the intent to affect the market and set forth substantial effect backing up their allegations. The defendants argued inter alia that the court should decline jurisdiction on international comity grounds because the laws of the United Kingdom permitted the anticompetitive conduct, whereas the Sherman Act prohibited it. The Supreme Court held that the comity exception was irrelevant since the persons subject to the regulation by the two states can comply with the laws of both states. Another layer to the extraterritorial application of the U.S. competition and merger laws was added in 2004 through the F. Hoffman-La Roche Ltd. case.[6] The case involved class actions seeking recovery for a worldwide conspiracy to fix price of vitamins. Put differently, vitamin purchasers filed a class action alleging that vitamin manufacturers and distributors had engaged in a price-fixing conspiracy, raising vitamin prices in the United States and foreign countries, in violation of the Sherman and Clayton Acts. The District Court applied the FTAIA and found none of its exceptions applicable. The Court of Appeals reversed, concluding that the FTAIA's exclusionary rule applied, but so did its exception for conduct that has a "direct, substantial and reasonably foreseeable effect" on domestic commerce that "gives rise to a Sherman Act claim." However, plaintiffs have developed and argued an alternative theory of the case, which was: the US effects did give rise to their claims because absent those effects, they would not have suffered injury.

[6] F. Hoffmann-La Roche Ltd. v. Empagran S.A., 542 U.S. 155, 164 (2004).

The U.S. Supreme Court held that:

> Where the price-fixing conduct significantly and adversely affects both customers outside and within the United States, but the adverse foreign effect is independent of any adverse domestic effect, the FTAIA exception does not apply, and thus, neither does the Sherman Act, to a claim based solely on the foreign effect.

The U.S. Supreme Court remanded the case to the Court of Appeals and required it to consider whether respondents properly preserved their alternative argument that the foreign injury was not in fact independent of the domestic effects; and, if so, the Court of Appeals may consider and decide the related claim.

6.2.2 U.S. Guidelines Under the U.S. Antitrust Laws[7]

The guidelines provide specific criteria concerning the extraterritorial application of U.S. antitrust law, including: (1) the relative significance of the alleged violation of conduct within the United States as compared to conduct abroad, (2) the degree of conflict with foreign national law, and (3) the effectiveness of foreign enforcement as compared with U.S. enforcement. The DOJ also has discretion in enforcing laws extraterritorially and can therefore determine whether to effectively bring conduct abroad within the scope of U.S. competition law. These guidelines provide a number of illustrative examples which assist in determining what constitutes a direct, substantial, and reasonably foreseeable effect. The determination of what constitutes a direct, substantial, and reasonably foreseeable effect is to be made on a case-by-case basis by the courts. However, an important indicia of a direct, substantial, and reasonably foreseeable effect is the elimination or significant reduction of competition in an appropriate market.[8]

[7] U.S. Department of Justice and Federal Trade Commission, Antitrust Enforcement Guidelines for International Operations, 4 Trade Reg. Rep. (CCH) ¶ 13,107 (1995).

[8] Richard W. Beckler (2003): Extraterritorial Application of U.S. Antitrust Law: What Is a "Direct, Substantial, and Reasonably Foreseeable Effect" Under the Foreign Trade Antitrust Improvements Act? *Texas International Law Review*, Vol. 38, No. 11, p. 19.

Illustrative Example C, Variant (1) of the Enforcement Guidelines states that a non-U.S. company that agrees outside the United States to price fix in a foreign country, with no intent to price fix in or otherwise affect the U.S. market, does not fall within the jurisdiction of subsection (1)(A) of the FTAIA.31 In this example, there is an agreement among non-U.S. companies to fix prices of materials sold in countries other than the United States with an explicit agreement that U.S. sales are outside the scope of the agreement. The agreement does enable cartel participants to charge less for their product in the United States—"several U.S. ... manufacturers curtail their production, overall domestic output falls, and remaining manufacturers fail to invest in new or improved capacity"—and thus causes an indirect effect on U.S. commerce. In addition, the anticompetitive cartel agreement could cause the price in the world market to stabilize or even rise, which also could indirectly affect U.S. prices. However, the guidelines provide that this conduct does not create the "direct, substantial, and reasonably foreseeable effect" necessary to trigger subject-matter jurisdiction under the FTAIA:

> The mere fact that the existence of U.S. sales or the level of U.S. prices may ultimately be affected by the cartel agreement is not enough for either Hartford Fire jurisdiction or the FTAIA. Furthermore, in the absence of an agreement with respect to the U.S. market, sales into the U.S. market at non-predatory levels do not raise antitrust concerns.

Variant (2) of Example C produces the opposite result. In this variant, "the cartel agreement specifically provides that cartel members will set agreed prices for the U.S. market at levels designed to soak up excess quantities that arise as a result of price increases in foreign markets." Here, according to the guidelines, subject-matter jurisdiction under subsection (1)(A) of the FTAIA exists:

> The critical element of a foreign price-fixing agreement with direct, intended effects in the U.S. is now present. The fact that the cartel believes its U.S. prices are "reasonable," or that it may be exerting downward pressure on U.S. price levels, does not exonerate it. Variant 2 presents a case where the Agencies would need clear evidence of the prohibited agreement before they would consider moving forward. They would be particularly cautious if the apparent effect in the U.S. market appeared to be beneficial to consumers.

- A direct effect

To establish a direct effect, a plaintiff must prove a specific link to anticompetitive effect within the United States for a court to exercise extraterritorial jurisdiction. In Phillips Petroleum Co., for instance, the United States District Court for the Southern District of Texas found that the foreign-based subsidiary of a U.S. corporation that sustained injuries abroad did not have a direct and substantial effect on U.S. commerce.[9] Likewise, conduct on American soil would not always be sufficient to prove effect on domestic commerce for it is the situs of the effect, not the conduct, which is determinative.

- The substantial effect

In defining what constitutes a substantial effect, some courts also focus on the size of the affected market and the relative harm of the anticompetitive foreign conduct.[10] Some courts have held that injury only to customers or potential customers located in a foreign nation and inconsequential injury to one U.S. export company was not sufficient for extraterritorial subject-matter jurisdiction.[11] Likewise, an allegation of mere monetary injury was not considered sufficient to create subject-matter jurisdiction.[12] However, in situations where there are a limited number of competitors in a given market, an injury to an individual may cause an injury to an entire market.[13] In Timberlane Lumber Co.,[14] the Ninth Circuit conducted an analysis of possible competing interests of different

[9] Phillips Petroleum Co. v. Heeremac, No. H-98-1698 (S.D. Tex. Jan. 22, 1999).

[10] Richard W. Beckler (2003): Extraterritorial Application of U.S. Antitrust Law: What Is a "Direct, Substantial, and Reasonably Foreseeable Effect" Under the Foreign Trade Antitrust Improvements Act? *Texas International Law Review*, Vol. 38, No. 11, p. 18.

[11] McGlinch v. Shell Chemical Co., 845 F.2d 802, 812–13 (9th Cir. 1988).

[12] McElderry v. Cathay Pacific, 678 F Suppl....

[13] Richard W. Beckler (2003): Extraterritorial Application of U.S. Antitrust Law: What Is a "Direct, Substantial, and Reasonably Foreseeable Effect" Under the Foreign Trade Antitrust Improvements Act? *Texas International Law Review*, Vol. 38, No. 11, p. 18.

[14] Timberlane Lumber Co. v. Bank of America, 549 F.2d 597 (9th Cir. 1976).

nations in determining whether the court should apply United States law or decline jurisdiction.[15] The facts of the case can be summed as follow:

- Timberlane Lumber Co., a United States corporation, had sought to establish lumber operations in Honduras for export to the United States.
- Timberlane Lumber Co., alleged, inter alia, that Bank of America, its affiliates, and others had conspired to prevent it from milling lumber in Honduras and exporting it to the United States.
- Due to the unfair competition environment (economic harassment), Timberlane Lumbe Co., ceased its operations.
- Timberlane alleged that such a conspiracy had a direct and substantial effect on U.S. Commerce under the Sherman Act.

In determining whether Timberland Lumber Co., had standing under the Sherman Act, Judge Choy promulgated a three-part test for extraterritorial applications of the Sherman Act: first, whether some effect, intended or unintended, on American commerce existed; second, whether United States antitrust law contemplated the particular restraint, in terms of magnitude and type, as a violation; and third, whether the United States' interests were sufficiently strong to justify an assertion of extraterritorial jurisdiction.

- The reasonably foreseeable effect

Sections 6a(1)(A) and (2) provide that the Sherman Act "shall not apply to conduct involving trade or commerce (other than import trade or import commerce) with foreign nations unless such conduct has a direct, substantial, and reasonably foreseeable effect on trade or commerce which is not trade or commerce with foreign nations, or on import trade or import commerce with foreign nations," and also, in either case, unless

[15] Evan Breibart (1989): The Wood Pulp Case: The Application of European Economic Community Competition Law to Foreign Based Undertakings, *Georgia Journal of International and Comparative Law*, p. 154.

the "effect [on import trade or domestic commerce] gives rise to a claim" under federal antitrust law.[16]

6.2.3 U.S. Extraterritorial Cases

6.2.3.1 The Ciba-Geigy and Sandoz Case

- The Federal Trade Commission initiated an investigation of the proposed merger between Ciba-Geigy Limited, including its wholly owned subsidiary Ciba-Geigy Corporation, and Sandoz Ltd., including its wholly owned subsidiary, Sandoz Corporation, into Novartis AG.
- The Commission aimed to remedy the alleged anticompetitive effects of the merger of Ciba-Geigy Limited and Sandoz Ltd. in several product markets, corn herbicides, flea control products, and various gene therapy markets.
- The Commission ordered that the merged firm, Novartis, divest the corn herbicide business and the flea control product business that belonged to Sandoz.
- Sandoz Ltd. was a corporation organized, and doing business under and by virtue of the laws of Switzerland with its office and principal place of business located at Lichtstrasse 35, CH-4002 Basel, Switzerland.
- Novartis AG, a company jointly formed by Ciba and Sandoz to effectuate the merger of Ciba and Sandoz through the acquisition of Ciba and Sandoz by Novartis. Novartis included Ciba and Sandoz; all of Novartis's directors, officers, employees, agents and representatives, predecessors, successors, and assigns; its subsidiaries, divisions, groups, and affiliates controlled, directly or indirectly, by Novartis AG; and the respective directors, officers, employees, agents and representatives, successors, and assigns of each.
- The FTC used its extraterritorial jurisdiction to enjoined divestiture, licensing of several specific IP to all interested parties.

[16] F. Hoffmann–La Roche Ltd. v. Empagran S.A., 542 U.S. 155, 161–62 (2004); Minn–Chem, Inc. v. Agrium, Inc., 683 F.3d 845, 853–54 (7th Cir. 2012) (en banc).

6.2.3.2 *The Motorola Mobility LLC Case*[17]

- Motorola (the plaintiff-appellant) and its ten foreign subsidiaries, bought liquid-crystal display (LCD) panels and incorporated them into cell phones manufactured by Motorola or the subsidiaries.
- Motorola accused foreign manufacturers of the panels of having violated Section 1 of the Sherman Act, by agreeing with each other on the prices they would charge for the panels.
- Motorola sought damages from companies over allegations that they fixed prices on LCD panels. Notably, some of the panels were manufactured in Asia, sold to Motorola subsidiaries in Asia, and then built into phones in Asia before being sold in the United States.
- The Korean Fair Trade Commission (KFTC) objected to U.S. jurisdiction over the transactions involving allegedly price-fixing products sold and delivered to Motorola's foreign subsidiaries, incorporated in mobile phones, and subsequently shipped to the United States.
- The Seventh Circuit threw out antitrust claims by Motorola, a U.S. company, against Asian electronics companies, concluding that the case had no place in a U.S. court.
- The Circuit Court held that:

> Motorola's foreign subsidiaries were injured in foreign commerce—in dealings with other foreign companies—and to give Motorola rights to take the place of its foreign companies and sue on their behalf under U.S. antitrust law would be an unjustified interference with the right of foreign nations to regulate their own economies. The foreign subsidiaries can sue under foreign law—are we to presume the inadequacy of the antitrust laws of our foreign allies?

6.3 Extraterritorial Competence of the EU Competition Laws

The European Union Merger Regulation, which came into force in 1990 and was revised in 2004, gives the European Commission the authority to review any concentration, which is deemed to have a "Community"

[17] Motorola Mobility LLC v. AU Optronics Corp., 775 F.3d 816 (7th Cir.), cert. denied, 135 S. Ct. 2837 (2015).

(in other words, an EU) dimension.[18] The Court of Justice of the EU has held the fact that an undertaking participating in an agreement is situated in a third country does not prevent the application of the TFEU if that agreement is operative on the territory of the internal market.[19] The Commission's external merger review relies on four key principles: (1) the exclusive competence of the Commission to review concentrations of Community dimension; (2) the mandatory notification of such concentrations; (3) the consistent application of market-oriented, competition-based criteria; and (4) the provision of legal certainty through timely decision-making.[20] A transaction is deemed to have an EU dimension if it meets either the original thresholds and/or the alternative thresholds.

- Original thresholds

Firms that receive annual revenues of 250 million euros (about $218 million) from operations in Europe, and combined global revenues of 5 billion euros (about $4.35 billion) are automatically subject to a review from the European Commission.

- Alternative thresholds

Under the alternative thresholds, a transaction would have an EU dimension if (1) the combined worldwide turnover of all the undertakings concerned exceeds €2500 or (2) each of at least two of the undertakings concerned [has] EU-wide turnover of more than €100 million or (3) if, in each of at least three EU Member States[,] the combined national turnover of all the undertakings concerned exceeds €100 million... and each of at least two of the undertakings concerned has a national turnover of more than 25 million.

[18] Council Regulation 139/2004 of 20 January 2004 on the Control of Concentrations between Undertakings, 2004 O.J. (L 24) 1 (EC) [hereinafter EC Merger Regulation].

[19] Working Party No. 3 on Co-operation and Enforcement Roundtable on the Extraterritorial Reach of Competition Remedies, p. 6.

[20] Council Regulation 139/2004 of 20 January 2004 on the Control of Concentrations between Undertakings, 2004 O.J. (L 24) 1 (EC) [hereinafter EC Merger Regulation].

6.3.1 The Enforcement Tools of Extraterritoriality

The exercise of extraterritorial competency is not easy. Strengthened international cooperation on the basis of bilateral agreements enables enforcement agencies to share case-related information, albeit subject to a number of limitations, conditions, and guarantees.[21] The ability to exchange information such as the "work product" of a competition enforcement agency. It covers the definition of the relevant product and geographic market, the agency's views on the nature of the anticompetitive behavior, as well as general nonpublic information relating to the conduct of the investigation, the possible targets, and the timing of dawn raids.[22]

6.3.2 EU Extraterritorial Cases

6.3.2.1 The Chemical Industries Case

In Chemical Industries case, the ECJ analyzed whether Article 81 EC (then Article 85 EC) was applicable to companies that were located and registered outside the EU, but that agreed to fix prices within the EC through their owned and controlled subsidiaries located within the EC. The Commission alleged that Imperial Chemical Industries, a foreign-registered undertaking, had engaged in concerted practices within the EC by dictating pricing instructions to its wholly owned subsidiary incorporated within the EC. In a three-prong theory, the EU Commission asserted that (i) ICI had actually been engaged in the concerted practices by dictating pricing to its EC-based subsidiary which acted merely as ICI's agent; (ii) ICI was present in the EC because of its corporate control over its subsidiary; and (iii) the activity of ICI produced effects within the Common Market.

The ECJ held that the anticompetitive effect of the price-fixing arrangements was felt in the EC. Hence, the ECJ held that the EC as the competition enforcement agency and guardian of the EC Treaty rightly asserted jurisdiction over such conduct. Regardless of whether the actual

[21] Georgios Kiriaziz: Jurisdiction and Cooperation Issues in the Investigation of International Cartels, DG COMP-A-4, p. 1.

[22] Georgios Kiriaziz: Jurisdiction and Cooperation Issues in the Investigation of International Cartels, DG COMP-A-4, p. 14.

anticompetitive conduct occurs outside the EC, if the effect of the conduct is to "affect trade between Member States" of the EC, such conduct will come within the reach of Articles 81 and 82 EC.

6.3.2.2 The Wood Pulp Case[23]

The Wood pulp judgment (regarding price fixing) confirmed that the Commission may extend its jurisdiction to cases in which an undertaking's conduct occurs outside the EU. In the 1985 Wood Pulp case, the ECJ came back to the question of extraterritorial application of EC competition law. The EC found that individual wood pulp producers and two associations of wood pulp producers had violated Article 85 of the Treaty of Rome by agreeing on prices that would be charged for their exports to the European Community. The EC imposed fines on wood pulp producers situated outside the EC for price-fixing arrangements contrary to Article 81 EC.

The EC argued that quarterly pre-disclosure announcements of prices from one company gave the other companies time to adjust their prices accordingly, leading to a concentration on prices. In asserting EC jurisdiction, the EC relied on the "effects" doctrine as in the Chemical Industries case and stated that Article 81 EC was applicable to conduct (even if such conduct is outside the EC or parties to the conduct are located abroad) that may affect trade between Member States. The Commission further argued that the effects in this case were substantial, direct, and intended. Although the companies in question had no subsidiaries within the EC, they exported their goods to the EC and about two-thirds of their shipments were affected by the agreement in question.

The ECJ articulated its reasoning on two key elements: (i) the existence of an agreement, decision, or concerted practice entered into by two or more undertakings, and (ii) the actual implementation within the EC of such an agreement. Implementation means the entering into a transaction or contract with a customer in the EC. As contracts were made with customers in the EC, the ECJ held that implementation took place within the EC; thus, the Commission rightly asserted EC jurisdiction.

[23] Cases 89/85, 114/85, 116–117/85, 125–129/85, a. Ahlstrom Osakeyhtid v. Commission (Wood Pulp) Decision of 27 September 1988.

> It should be observed that an infringement of Article 85, such as the conclusion of an agreement which has had the effect of restricting competition within the Common Market, consists of conduct made up of two elements, the formation of the agreement, decision or concerted practice and the implementation thereof.... The producers in this case implemented their pricing agreement within the Common Market It is immaterial in that respect whether or not they had recourse to subsidiaries, agents, sub-agents, or branches within the Community in order to make their contracts with purchasers within the Community. Accordingly the Community's jurisdiction to apply its competition rules to such conduct is covered by the territoriality principle as universally recognized in public international law.[24]

6.3.2.3 Gencor Ltd. v. Commission[25]

The Gencor case confirmed that the application of the EUMR to concentrations of undertakings conducting operations outside the EU is consistent with the EUMR and public international law "when it is foreseeable that a proposed concentration will have an immediate and substantial effect" in the EU.[26] The case, which was handled by the Court of First Instance (CFI), concerned the merger between Gencor, a South African company, and Lonrho, a British company, which would have allowed them to control a large share of the world market of platinum, rhodium, and related metals, leaving only one substantial competitor and thus resulting in the creation of an oligopoly. The EC held that the merger could negatively affect the common market by restricting the output of these materials and leading to upward pressure on prices. The CFI referred to the principle of "extended territoriality" to hold that "application of the regulation is justified under public international law when it is foreseeable that the proposed concentration will have an immediate and substantial effect in the community." It is noteworthy to see that the CFI referred to an "immediate and substantial effect" in the European Union, which effectively aligned the European Union's reasoning with the effects doctrine in the United States.

[24] Paras. 16, 17, 18.

[25] Case T-102/96, Gencor Ltd. v. Comm'n, 1999 E.C.R. II-753, 761–62.

[26] OECD (2017): Working Party No. 3 on Co-operation and Enforcement Roundtable on the Extraterritorial Reach of Competition Remedies, p. 6.

6.3.2.4 *Boeing McDonnell Douglas*

In December 1996, the Seattle-based company Boeing announced its intention to acquire its biggest U.S. competitor, St. Louis-based McDonnell Douglas. After the merger, Boeing would become the sole American manufacturer of commercial … aircraft[s].

Boeing held a share of about 60 percent in the global civil aircraft market, and the proposed merger would have left Airbus as its only remaining rival.

- On July 1, 1997, the FTC announced that McDonnell Douglas was "no longer in a position to influence significantly the competitive dynamics of the commercial aircraft market," so the merger posed no threat to competition.
- In May 1997, the European Commission issued a statement of objections on the proposed merger. The European Commission particularly feared that Boeing would have an increased ability to negotiate with customers for exclusive supply agreements, thus limiting foreign competitors from important segments of the worldwide market. Following the EC's objections, negotiations took place resulting in important concessions, inter alia, Boeing agreed to terminate its exclusive supply contract with three carriers.
- On July 27, 1997, once these conditions were met, the EC approved the merger.

6.3.2.5 *Google/Motorola*[27]

- On November 25, 2011, the European Commission received notification of a proposed concentration pursuant to Article 4 of Council Regulation No 139/20041 by which Google Inc. ("Google", USA), acquired, within the meaning of Article 3(1)(b) of the Merger Regulation, sole control over Motorola Mobility Holdings, Inc. ("Motorola Mobility", USA) by way of purchase of shares.
- Google is a provider of internet search and online advertising services. It also provides a number of additional online services and software products. Google's revenue is mostly derived from online advertising services and, to a certain extent, from mobile online advertising services. Google also develops and makes available

[27] Google/Motorola Mobility, case No. COMP/M.6381.

to original equipment manufacturers ("OEMs") of smart mobile devices an open source mobile operating system ("OS") called Android. Google is the leading member of the Open Handset Alliance ("OHA").

- Motorola Mobility is a supplier of mobile devices (including smart mobile devices), TV set-top boxes (STBs), end-to-end video solutions, and cable broadband access solutions.
- Pursuant to the Agreement and Plan of Merger signed on August 15, 2011, Google will acquire the whole of Motorola Mobility by way of purchase of shares via its fully owned subsidiary RB98 Inc., a Delaware corporation. The transaction will result in the acquisition of sole control by Google over Motorola Mobility and thus constitutes a concentration pursuant to Article 3(1)(b) of the Merger Regulation.
- Google submitted that it would acquire approximately [7000–8000] patents ([6000–7000] US and [500–1000] EU patents) from Motorola Mobility, which focused mainly on wireless communication hardware and to some extent high-definition television ("HDTV").
- The parties to the proposed transaction had a combined aggregate worldwide turnover of more than EUR 5000 million (EUR 20,941 million for Google and EUR 8644 million for Motorola Mobility). Each had an EU-wide turnover in excess of EUR 250 million (EUR [...] million for Google and EUR [...] million for Motorola Mobility) and neither achieved more than two-thirds of its aggregate EU-wide turnover within one and the same Member State.
- The notified operation therefore had an EU dimension.
- The notifying party submitted that the transaction will bring together two complementary businesses and does not give rise to any horizontally or vertically affected markets.
- While the parties' activities horizontally overlapped to a limited extent in the market for conditional access systems, their combined market share was significantly less than 15% ([5–10]% worldwide and [0–5]% in the EEA based on the party's estimates).
- As a result, the transaction does not give rise to any horizontally affected markets.
- Nevertheless, given the vertical relationships between Google as the supplier of the open source Android OS and online services on the

one hand and Motorola Mobility as a supplier of mobile devices and holder of important Intellectual Property Rights for mobile devices on the other hand, the Commission has analyzed the possible effects on competition resulting from these vertical relationships.

- Google submitted that there was a single product market for mobile software platforms for smartphones and mobile software platforms for tablets, arguing that there were no significant supply-side constraints that prevent a mobile software platform running on a smartphone from running on a tablet, as both types of devices provide similar capabilities and use very similar hardware configurations.
- The Commission noted that the majority of respondents to the market investigation considered that OSs for PCs and OSs for smart mobile devices belong to separate product markets given that both use different hardware and have different performance capacities.
- Concerning the geographic market, Google argued that the geographic scope of the market should therefore be considered to be worldwide, and the Commission agreed that the relevant geographic market for mobile OS is at least EEA-wide, or even worldwide, in scope.
- Likewise, the Commission determined that, for mobile devices, the relevant markets were the markets for smart mobile devices (whether further differentiated according to smartphones and tablets respectively) on an EEA-wide or worldwide basis.
- After that, the Commission went on to analyze the vertical, horizontal, and conglomerate effects of the deal.

• Vertical relation

- Google claimed that it did not control Android and therefore Android's market share ([40–50]% of smart mobile devices in the EEA currently run on Android) should not be attributed to Google but to each of the various OEMs building Android based phones.
- The Commission did not accept Google's view that Android's market share cannot be attributed to it for some specific reasons.[28]

[28] (i) Google owned the IPR to the Android mobile OS, (ii) Google was responsible for releasing each new version of the Android mobile OS, (iii) Google effectively had to approve each smartphone or tablet running on Android which was built as an Android

- Consequently, the Commission concluded that Google controls Android and all of the market share corresponding to Android should be attributed to Google.
- Furthermore, the Commission analyzed the post-transaction effects of the merger, and found that Google would become a vertically integrated producer of smart mobile devices. To that end, the Commission examined (i) whether the merged entity would post-merger have the ability to substantially foreclose access to input; (ii) whether the merged entity would have the incentive to do so; and (iii) whether a foreclosure strategy would give rise to a significant impediment to effective competition downstream.
- Google stated that it had no incentive to start favoring Motorola Mobility given Motorola Mobility's minute share in the EEA ([0–5]%). Google had pointed out that its revenue comes largely from online and mobile advertising. Therefore, restricting access to the Android ecosystem would most likely cause Google a significant loss in the advertising revenue associated with Google search and other applications and services (all Android partners preinstall these Google products on their smart mobile devices). Given Motorola Mobility's very low market share, the revenue loss for Google from restricting access to Android is most likely to be far greater than the potential gain from Motorola Mobility smart mobile device sales.
- Moreover, Google specified that the rationale for the transaction did not reside in the acquisition of Motorola Mobility's mobile device hardware business but rather in the acquisition of Motorola Mobility's patent portfolio. The transaction had been widely welcomed by industry participants.
- The Commission agreed that Google was unlikely to have the incentives to restrict third-party OEMs access to Android as it was doubtful that Google could, in the short to medium term, capture more profits by favoring Motorola Mobility's smart mobile devices rather than through having a large base for its search and advertising services.

device and had to approve the implementation of its applications on devices that ship with Google applications preinstalled, (iv) even though the source code for the Android mobile OS was released by Google for free under an open source licence, Android OEMs still remained highly dependent on Google, and (v) a Google internal document showed that Google exerted control over Android.

- The Commission went on to say that, even, assuming arguendo that Google were to prevent Motorola Mobility's competitors from accessing Android or were to degrade the versions of Android offered to competing OEMs, a significant impediment to effective competition is unlikely to arise.
- The Commission determined that Google was unlikely to have the incentive to foreclose OEMs from access to Android post-merger as even if it did attempt to foreclose Motorola Mobility's competitors from accessing Android, competing OEMs would have alternatives to which they could turn.
- Considering the possibility that Google would be in a position to foreclose access to Motorola Mobility's smart mobile devices to competing mobile OS suppliers, the Commission determined that significant competition concerns with regard to customer foreclosure were unlikely to arise.
- Concerning the intellectual right effects of the transfer of Motorola Mobility's SEP to Google, the Commission investigated whether Google would have the ability and incentive to use Motorola Mobility's SEPs in a way which would raise serious doubts as to the merger's compatibility with the internal market.
- Google argued that going forward, it would be constrained by the FRAND commitment which has been given by Motorola Mobility.
- The Commission determined that though Google might have some ability to use its SEPs to significantly impede effective competition post-merger, in particular through seeking and enforcing injunctions, it was unlikely that Google would do so. That Google would be bound by Motorola Mobility's FRAND commitment with respect to its SEPs and considers that this would constrain Google's incentives to raise the royalty level.
- The Commission also found that Google's incentives to threaten, seek, and/or enforce injunctions against good faith prospective licensees in order to force cross-licences for technology that the counter party would not otherwise wish to license, were limited.
- For all the above reasons, the Commission concluded that the proposed transaction did not raise serious doubts as to its compatibility with the internal market with respect to Google's acquisition of Motorola Mobility's IP rights, including Motorola Mobility's SEPs.

- Conglomerate relation

- In addition to the vertical relationships afore-examined, the Commission considered it appropriate to examine the conglomerate relationship between, on the one hand, Motorola Mobility's smart mobile devices and IP rights and, on the other hand, Google's mobile online services.
- Motorola Mobility and Google were therefore active on markets that were, to some extent, related. Motorola Mobility's products and some of Google's products could be considered complementary or to belong to a range of products that was generally consumed by the same set of customers for the same end use, namely consumers that used smartphones or tablets.
- To that end, the Commission considered that, to the extent that there were OEMs with whom Motorola Mobility had not entered into cross-licensing agreements, Google would have the ability to contractually tie or bundle the licence for Motorola Mobility's SEPs with the use of Google's mobile services.
- The Commission found Google's ability to tie/bundle Motorola Mobility's SEPs and Google mobile services towards Android OEMs (who do not already have licences for Motorola Mobility's SEPs) already existed in practice pre-merger through a web of agreements. Therefore, Google's merger-specific ability to impose Google services on OEMs and MNOs stemming from the proposed transaction was limited.

For all the above reasons, the Commission found that Google's proposed acquisition of Motorola Mobility did not raise serious doubts as to its compatibility with the internal market on the basis of conglomerate effects.

6.3.2.6 General Electric/Honeywell[29]

- General Electric Company "a diversified corporation active in fields including aircraft engines, appliances, information services, power

[29] Commission Decision COMP/M.2220—General Electric/Honeywell, 2001 O.J. (L.48) 1 (EC).

systems, lighting, industrial systems, medical systems, plastics, broadcasting (through the NBC media channel), financial services and transportation systems."

- Honeywell International Inc. "an advanced technology and manufacturing company serving customers worldwide with aerospace products and services, automotive products, electronic materials, specialty chemicals, performance polymers, transportation and power systems [and] home, building and industrial controls."
- In October 2000, Honeywell (then valued at over $21 billion) accepted a takeover bid from then-CEO Jack Welch of General Electric. Honeywell and GE were both industrial conglomerates, but their product lines had few overlaps. The $42 billion merger of the two U.S. companies had already received regulatory approval in the United States with the recommendation that GE divest itself of Honeywell's military helicopter unit, to protect the U.S. military.
- The U.S. Justice Department approved the takeover, ruling that GE's and Honeywell's product ranges were mostly complementary—that is, the two companies did not make the same things and hence were not competitors. But what was approved by the US DOJ would not receive the blessing or approval of the European Commission. The European Commission task force therefore insisted that GE sell off Honeywell's avionics business or detach its own subsidiary, GE Capital Aviation Services, which finances aerospace purchases. GE offered some concessions but not enough for the European Commission.
- The European Commission found that such a merger would have adverse effects on the competitive position in the aerospace industry. That is, the merger would give the two companies a very huge combined market shares in the common markets in which they operated, along with providing them with the opportunity to bundle their complementary products in future.
- The Commission was concerned that strength of the combined positions of the merging firms would allow GE to engage in exclusionary product bundling[30] with the ultimate effect of foreclosing markets

[30] Its avionics (e.g. aircraft communication and navigation equipment) and non-avionics products (e.g. wheels, lights and landing gear) with engines, at a discount to single product purchases, which competitors could not match.

for single product line competitors (particularly Rolls-Royce in aircraft engines and Rockwell Collins in aerospace components). Such foreclosure involved the deterrence of new entrants, the reduction of investment by existing competitors, and possibly their exit.[31] This would harm competitors as well as customers by creating a near monopoly situation.

- Among the challengers of the merger, Rolls-Royce stressed the dangers of allowing GE to "bundle" engines and avionics in packages that other firms could not match, and United Technologies concentrated on GE's role as a buyer of planes through GE Capital Aviation Services, its finance, and leasing subsidiary.
- The European Commission also received evidence from aerospace component competitors (in particular Rockwell Collins) that they had faced Honeywell component bundling, and were unable to compete.[32]
- The EC believed that the combination of Honeywell's cockpit controls with GE's engines and powerful aircraft financing division would stifle competition. In other words, it viewed with suspicion precisely those synergies that, for Welch, made the deal so attractive. The European Commission would approve the merger only if GE agreed to sell $4 billion of its avionics business to competitors. But, Welch was reluctant to make the kind of concessions that, from GE's standpoint, wrecked its whole point. Nonetheless, GE unveiled an eleventh-hour counter proposal, offering to sell 19.9% of GECAS in a private placement to noncompetitors. That also was not enough to address the European Commission concerns.
- On June 28, 2001, European Commission officials voted to endorse Monti's recommendation that the merger be rejected. The Commission also found that the merging parties had not provided any efficiencies as a justification for the transaction. Indeed, the efficiencies' analysis aim to entice and convince the Commission to distinguish between a merger that strengthens a company's market position through efficiencies that ultimately benefit consumer welfare, from a merger whose main purpose is to enable the combined entity

[31] Jeremy Grant (2005): *The Attempted Merger Between General Electric and Honeywell: A Case Study of Transatlantic Conflict*, Graduate Institute of International Studies, Geneva, p. 4.

[32] Testimony given at Honeywell appeal hearing, Luxembourg, May 25, 2004.

to implement anticompetitive conduct including possibly predatory behavior, with the effect of marginalizing and ultimately driving its competitors from the market.

> This merger, as it was notified, would have severely reduced competition in the aerospace industry and resulted, ultimately, in higher prices for customers, particularly airlines.

- The European Commission veto was later upheld by the European Court of First Instance. However, the European Court criticized the antitrust regulator's argument that bundling the groups' products together would have allowed the combined company to dominate parts of the aerospace sector.
- The difference between the DOJ and the European Commission laid on their respective aims: the European Commission focused on the effects that a proposed merger would have on the competition, while U.S. antitrust officials concentrated on the effects it would have on consumers.[33]
- The GE case was considered extraordinary. Never before have officials outside the United States nixed a merger between two giant American corporations already approved by the DOJ.

6.4 Extraterritorial Competence of China's AML

In China, the extended territorial application of the AML is laid down under Article 2 which deals with the scope of its application. Article 2 of the AML states:

> This Law is applicable to monopolistic conducts in economic activities within the territory of the People's Republic of China; and it is applicable to monopolistic conducts outside the territory of the People's Republic of China, which serve to eliminate or restrict competition on the domestic market of China.

[33](2001): Lessons from the GE-Honeywell Non-Merger, knowledge.wharton.upenn.edu.

Article 2 of the AML provides for an extraterritorial doctrine effect. However, neither China's legislature nor its enforcement agencies have promulgated specific regulations thereon.[34]

6.4.1 *The Enforcement Tools of Extraterritoriality*

China's enforcement tools of extraterritoriality comply with international laws, and the enforcement agencies are heavily involved in bilateral agreement with both the US (DOJ) and the European Commission.

6.4.2 *China Extraterritorial Cases*

In the following cases, while the transactions had global effects, only China—MOFCOM—imposed conditions after review.[35]

6.4.2.1 *The Silvinit/Uralkali Case*[36]

- Uralkali, a major potash, or potassium chloride, producer based in Russia, proposed to acquire Uralkali, another Russian potash producer. Potash is a key fertilizer ingredient and China is one of the largest potash consuming nations, with growing demand that is about 50% satisfied by imports.
- MOFCOM found that the relevant product market is potassium chloride, a major form of potassium fertilizer as well as a key ingredient in other types of fertilizers, and considered the global and domestic market for potassium chloride, including imports into China.
- The production of potassium chloride depends on the availability of potassium. The majority of known potassium reserves are located in three countries, with production and sales of potassium chloride concentrated in a few companies.

[34] Zhan Hao, Song Yin, and Stephanie Wu (2019): Global Legal Insights, Cartel 2019-China.

[35] Yee Wah Chin (2012): *M&A Under China's Anti-Monopoly Laws*, Victoria University of Wellington Law School.

[36] MOFCOM Announcement [2011] no. 33 regarding the Anti-Monopoly Review Decision for Conditional Clearance of the Combination of Joint Stock Company Uralkali with Joint Stock Company Silvinit, http://fldj.mofcom.gov.cn/aarticle/zcfb/201106/20110607583288.html (in Chinese) (visited February 17, 2012).

- MOFCOM found that the Uralkali/Silvinit combination would be the world's second largest potassium chloride exporter, accounting for over one-third of global exports. The combination, together with the largest supplier, would account for approximately 70% of world potassium chloride supply. About half of China's potassium chloride imports are from Uralkali, Silvinit and their affiliates, with about 1/3 of China's potassium chloride imports being border trades with Uralkali and Silvinit.
- MOFCOM found high barriers to entry to the potassium chloride market, since known reserves are concentrated in existing producers and developing or expanding mines require substantial resources, with substantial risks.
- MOFCOM concluded that the transaction would increase concentration in the relevant market and may adversely affect competition in international trade of potassium chloride, as well as raise the likelihood of coordinated anticompetitive conduct by potassium chloride suppliers. Apparently distinguishing a geographic market of border trades (versus ocean shipping) of potassium chloride, it concluded that the combination of Uralkali and Silvinit may exclude or restrict competition in border trades of potassium chloride. Notably, MOFCOM concluded that, in light of China's reliance on potassium chloride imports and the current potassium chloride market structure, the transaction would affect China's agriculture and other relevant industries.

In order to mitigate the adverse impact on competition in the Chinese market for potassium chloride, MOFCOM approved the transaction on conditions that Uralkali/Silvinit:

(i) Maintain current sales practices, and continue to sell potassium chloride directly to the Chinese market and to use its utmost best efforts to provide reliable and stable supplies of potassium chloride to China by rail and sea.
(ii) Continue to supply a full line of potassium chloride products in sufficient quantities to the Chinese market, including KCl products with 60% and 62% potassium oxide (encompassing white potassium [chloride] and pink/red potassium [chloride]), as well to

supply its Chinese customers, satisfying the volume and types of their needs for all uses.
(iii) Continue its customary negotiation processes, fully factoring in the history of dealings with Chinese customers and current circumstances as well as the special characteristics of the Chinese market in price negotiations, which include spot sales and contract sales.
(iv) Report semiannually or as MOFCOM requests on compliance with the decision, and appoint a monitoring trustee to supervise performance of the obligations.

MOFCOM will inspect, monitor, and oversee compliance with the conditions, and may penalize noncompliance.

The decision reflects understandable concern with assuring secure supply of what might be considered a strategic resource. On the other hand, the conditions imposed would seem to handicap what would be the second largest supplier, leaving the largest supplier possibly at a greater competitive advantage, which would appear to be antithetical to the goals of competition law. From the enforcement perspective, the general language of the decision provides MOFCOM with great discretion in determining compliance.

6.4.2.2 *The Savio Macchine Tessili S.P.A Case*[37]

- Alpha Private Equity Fund V, a French private equity fund and the largest shareholder in Uster Technologies Co. Ltd., with a 27.9% equity position, sought to acquire Savio Macchine Tessili S.P.A through a newly created subsidiary Penelope Co. Ltd. Savio is the parent of Loepfe Bros. Ltd.
- Uster, a public Swiss company, and Loepfe are the only two manufacturers in the world of electronic yarn clearers for automatic winders, accounting for 52.3% and 47.7%, respectively, of the world and Chinese markets. An electronic yarn clearer detects and repairs yarn defects at high speed during the manufacturing process.

[37] MOFCOM Announcement [2011] no. 73 Regarding anti-monopoly review decision granting conditional approval of the acquisition by Penelope Company Ltd. of Savio Macchine Tessili S.P.A, http://fldj.mofcom.gov.cn/aarticle/zcfb/201111/20111107809156.html?149782665=840603354 (in Chinese) (visited February 17, 2012).

- MOFCOM determined that electronic yarn clearers for automatic winders is a distinct relevant market.
- MOFCOM found that intellectual property rights is a significant barrier to entry into electronic yarn clearers for automatic winders. Moreover, economies of scale are important and difficult to achieve quickly for new entrants. There have been no successful new entrants in the last three years, although there were efforts in 2009 to introduce new electronic yarn clearers that had gained little customer acceptance by 2010.
- MOFCOM focused on the control that Alpha V might exert on Uster, and investigated Uster's shareholders' holdings, shareholder voting rights, historic attendance at shareholders' meetings, board composition, and governance. It concluded that there was a possibility of Alpha V influencing Uster's operations. MOFCOM found that the transaction is likely to result in Uster and Loepfe coordinating through Alpha V and Alpha V restricting or eliminating competition through its control and influence over Uster and Loepfe. Therefore, MOFCOM concluded that the transaction would or may restrict or eliminate competition in the market for electronic yarn clearers for automatic winders.
- MOFCOM conditioned approval of the acquisition of Savio on the divestiture within six months of the 27.9% holding in Uster. A monitoring trustee is to supervise the divestiture pursuant to the Provisional Regulations regarding Divestitures in Concentrations and the buyer, price and date for the sale is to be reported to MOFCOM. In the meantime, Alpha V and its ultimate parent may not participate in or influence Uster's management. MOFCOM may monitor and audit compliance with the conditions.

6.4.2.3 *The GE–Shenhua Case*[38]

- The GE–Shenhua Joint Venture was established by General Electric (China) Co. Ltd. and China Shenhua Coal to Liquid and Chemical

[38] MOFCOM Announcement [2011] no. 74 regarding the Anti-Monopoly Review Decision for Conditional Clearance of Contemplated Joint Venture between General Electric (China) Co. Ltd. and China Shenhua Coal to Liquid and Chemical Co. Ltd., http://fldj.mofcom.gov.cn/aarticle/zcfb/201111/20111107824342.html?1104118153=840603354 (in Chinese) (visited February 16, 2012).

Co. Ltd., a subsidiary of the state-owned Shenhua Group Corporation Limited, to develop a coal-water slurry gasification technology and a licensing program for the technology in China. The technology transforms coal into a coal-water slurry and then into a mixture of gasses. GE would license its coal-water slurry gasification technology to the JV while CSCLC contributes its expertise in coal gasification and coal-fired power generation. The formation of the JV was announced in January 2011, during President Hu Jintao's visit to the United States.

- A notification under the AML was submitted to MOFCOM on April 13, 2011, and was accepted on May 16, after supplementation. MOFCOM's review went into Phase 3 before a decision was issued on November 10, 2011.
- MOFCOM found that coal-water slurry gasification technology is significantly different from other coal gasification technologies in its requirements for raw materials and methods. The Shenhua Group, which includes CSCLS, is the largest supplier in China of the type of coal suitable for coal-water slurry gasification. MOFCOM also found that domestic customers for the technology sourced the technology only from suppliers within China. There are only three major suppliers of the technology in China, with GE holding the largest market share, and the two other being Chinese entities. Entry barriers are high for other coal-water slurry technology, since it is complex and requires substantial engineering expertise to master, so that there are significant commercial risks for new technologies. It is an area covered by many patents that requires substantial start up time and investment. A new technology would generally need to find a user that is willing to underwrite some of the costs of the prototype. As a result, a new technology faces significant challenges in being licensed.
- Therefore, MOFCOM concluded that the JV is likely to restrict or eliminate competition in the licensing of coal-water slurry gasification technology in China, being a combination of the largest supplier of raw coal for coal-water slurry gasification and the largest supplier of coal slurry gasification technology. It found that the JV may leverage Shenhua's position in raw coal and control its supply.
- As conditions for approving the formation of the JV, GE China, and CSCLC are prohibited from forcing technology customers to use the JV's technology or raising the costs of using other technologies,

by restricting the supply of raw coal for use with coal-water slurry gasification technology or by conditioning the license of the JV's technology on the supply of raw coal. MOFCOM would monitor compliance with the restriction.

- MOFCOM's decision is significant because it is the first involving a SOE and a JV. The facts that the GE–Shenhua JV was announced by China's President and involved a SOE, but still went into Phase 3, may reflect MOFCOM's assertion of independence from noncompetition considerations in its merger reviews.
- MOFCOM concern derives from the vertical relationship between the Shenhua Group, with its control of raw materials, and the JV with technology that processes those raw materials. While MOFCOM noted that Shenhua is the largest supplier of raw coal for use in coal-water slurry gasification, without information as to the size of other suppliers, it's unclear that Shenhua's market position in raw coal is so large as to raise concerns under U.S. antitrust standards about exclusion of downstream competitors to the JV's technology or raising the costs of using downstream competing technology.

6.4.2.4 *The Seagate/Samsung Case*[39]

- MOFCOM's decision conditionally approving Seagate's acquisition of Samsung's hard disk drive business is by far its longest and most detailed to date, reflecting a considerable amount of economic analysis. In contrast, both the EU and the U.S. enforcement authorities cleared the transaction unconditionally.
- MOFCOM found that HDDs are distinguishable from other storage media such as solid state drives and flash drives in terms of capacity, price, and use, and that HDDs comprise a product market. It recognized that HDDs have different end uses and may be divided into submarkets such as HDDs for servers, desktop computers, laptop computers, and consumer electronics. The relevant geographic market is global as the supply and sale of HDD are carried out worldwide.

[39] MOFCOM Announcement no. 90 (2011) regarding anti-monopoly review decision granting conditional approval of Seagate Technology LLC acquisition of Samsung Electronics Co. Ltd. hard disk drive business, http://fldj.mofcom.gov.cn/aarticle/zcfb/201112/20111207874274.html?3102376073=840603354 (in Chinese) (visited February 17, 2012).

- Market concentration has increased in the last 20 years, so that there are only five HDD manufacturers worldwide: Seagate, Western Digital, Hitachi Storage, Toshiba, and Samsung. Their share of global and China sales were approximately 33%, 29%, 18%, 10%, and 10%, respectively. The HDD market is fairly transparent. MOFCOM considered HDDs to be commodities and their manufacturers to be fairly undifferentiated in their product lines. Customers can readily switch suppliers. There are relatively few major buyers, and manufacturers often have common distributors to market to other buyers. Prices paid by the major buyers, the large computer manufacturers, generally set market prices. HDD manufacturers can therefore fairly readily discern competitors' technology, costs, prices, output, and sales.
- Major computer makers often use confidential bidding for HDD procurement, with quarterly bilateral negotiations with HDD makers. To ensure continuity and security of supply, the computer makers generally divide their purchases among 2–4 HDD makers, allocating the purchase volumes according to the prices and other terms and conditions of sale offered. In each round of negotiations, the most competitive HDD maker will get the largest order, while the least may get none. This process requires HDD makers to compete. MOFCOM concluded that maintaining the current procurement process is crucial to maintaining competition in the HDD market.
- On the other hand, MOFCOM found that large computer makers generally are indifferent to price increases that are not targeted towards any particular customer, because they can pass on the increases in the computers sold to consumers, who are dispersed and have no countervailing buying power. HDD makers generally direct pricing for distributors and distributors have insufficient purchasing power to resist the HDD makers. MOFCOM noted that Western Digital's loss of substantial production capacity from recent floods in Thailand led to HDD price increases by all manufacturers, and price increases in computers that apparently resulted from computer makers passing on those HDD price increases.
- MOFCOM also found that capacity usage in HDD manufacturing has been increasing steadily since 2008, with about 90% usage in the fourth quarter of 2010. Innovation is a major factor in the

HDD industry, with profit margins dropping quickly as an innovation spreads through the industry, so that manufacturers have constantly sought to reduce costs through innovation.

- MOFCOM concluded that competition is a major driver of innovation in the HDD industry and any reduction of competition would substantially reduce the motivation for and speed of innovation on the part of manufacturers.
- Moreover, the substantial intellectual property and technical expertise needed to establish a HDD manufacturing facility is a substantial barrier to entry. Economies of scale in HDD manufacturing and the large minimum viable scale of a HDD facility also present huge risks and barriers to entry. There have been no new entrants into HDD manufacturing in the last 10 years. MOFCOM concluded that it is difficult to enter the HDD market.
- MOFCOM found that the transaction would eliminate a major competitor, reduce competitive pressure on the remaining HDD makers, and enhance their ability to obtain purchase orders under the prevailing bidding process. Given the relative transparency of the HDD market, which already enables HDD makers to predict competitors' behavior, the transaction will enhance their potential for coordinated action to restrict or exclude competition. MOFCOM noted that China is one of the major personal computer consumer nations and concluded that the transaction would adversely affect Chinese consumers. It would exclude and restrict competition in the HDD market.

As a result, MOFCOM imposed the following conditions:

(i) Samsung will be maintained as an independent competitor, including by (a) establishing a new Seagate subsidiary to independently price Samsung's existing HDD product line ("Samsung Products") and independently market the Samsung HDD brand, with both Seagate and Samsung sales teams reporting to and under the supervision of the monitoring trustee, (b) having Samsung's existing sales staff continue to sell Samsung Products during the transition in ways that will not jeopardize the competitiveness of those products, and report sales to and be supervised by the monitoring trustee, (c) maintaining the pricing independence of the

Samsung sales team, with a firewall to prevent exchange of competitive information between the Samsung and Seagate teams, with only one designated Samsung sales person reporting to only one designated Seagate person, only on noncompetitive matters, with the identities of both to be reported in advance to the monitoring trustee and the substance of any communications between them to be reported simultaneously or in advance to the trustee and subject to the trustee's supervision, (d) maintaining independent operation of Samsung's production line, with Samsung's equipment, processes and production system, and technical support and innovation to improve the productivity and competitiveness of Samsung Products that is reported to the monitoring trustee throughout and subject to the trustee's supervision, (e) establishing an independent reasonable pricing mechanism for Samsung Products under the supervision of the monitoring trustee, and (f) establishing an independent R&D center for Samsung Products, with technical support from Seagate including Seagate's standard processes to improve the capacity and competitiveness of Samsung Products, all reported to and under supervision of the monitoring trustee.

(ii) Seagate will maintain and expand the capacity of Samsung Products within 6 months, and thereafter set the capacity and volume of Samsung Products reasonably according to market demand conditions. The capacity and volume of Samsung and Seagate products shall be reported monthly to the monitoring trustee.

(iii) Seagate may not substantively change its current business model, or expressly or implicitly require customers to purchase HDDs exclusively from Seagate or any entities it controls.

(iv) Seagate may not require TDK China Co. Ltd. to supply HDD heads exclusively to Seagate or any entities it controls, or limit the volume of HDD heads that TDK may supply to other HDD manufacturers.

(v) Seagate will invest at least $800 million annually for 3 years, and fund R&D in innovation at rates comparable to that in recent years, to ensure providing customers even more innovative products and solutions.

(vi) Seagate will appoint a monitoring trustee pursuant to the Provisional Regulations regarding Divestitures in Concentrations, to supervise its compliance with the conditions.

- MOFCOM also provided that, after 12 months, Seagate may seek release from the first 2 conditions. Seagate must submit an implementation plan within a week of appointing the monitoring trustee, and MOFCOM will monitor Seagate's performance.
- MOFCOM apparently put little if any weight on the facts that a growing number of computers have no hard disk drives, different size disk drives are not interchangeable in their end use, and it is a significant adjustment to switch HDD production from one size to another.

In contrast, the European Commission concluded that there were several HDD markets worldwide, based on their end uses.[40] It found that the primary impact of the transaction would be in 2 HDD markets in which Samsung was not a particularly strong competitor, leaving 3 strong competitors in 3.5″ desktop computer HDDs and 4 strong competitors in 2.5″ mobile equipment HDDs, so that customers would have sufficient alternative suppliers. The EC also found that the removal of Samsung is unlikely to create a risk of coordination among the remaining HDD makers. Moreover, it concluded that TDK would still be able to sell a sufficient volume of HDD heads to the combined Seagate/Samsung to be a viable business.

MOFCOM seems to have reached inconsistent conclusions in finding that computer makers make use of a sophisticated system to ensure the most economic yet secure supply of a crucial input, HDDs, but have little incentive to resist price increases. MOFCOM may have misread the ability of computer manufacturers to pass on cost increases to consumers. It may also have reached an inapt conclusion from the market reaction to the shortage caused by the Thai floods. The price increase following the floods more likely reflect the natural interactions of supply and demand, not any exercise or lack of market power.

[40] Press Release IP/11/1213, October 19, 2011, http://europa.eu/rapid/pressReleasesAction.do?reference=IP/11/1213.

CHAPTER 7

Cooperation Among the Three Jurisdictions

7.1 General

An increasing number of mergers, IJV has a cross-border dimension that lead to multiple jurisdiction interventions. Currently, the United States, the EU, Japan, and China have asserted extraterritorial competency over mergers with significant impacts over their respective economies. To that end, an effective cooperation between competition authorities is more than important. The OECD/ICN[1] Survey confirmed an increase in the use of international cooperation over the five-year period, with an estimated increase of approximately 15% in the number of cartel cases requiring some form of international cooperation, 35% in merger review cases, and 30% in unilateral conduct cases.[2] The purpose of international enforcement cooperation is twofold: (i) cooperation offers authorities the opportunity to have more effective investigations and to generate efficiencies, (ii) cooperation aims at minimizing risks of divergent outcomes by facilitating the dialogue among the enforcers involved in the review of the same case[3] (Fig. 7.1).

[1] ICN: International Competition Network.

[2] OECD (2014): Challenges of International Co-operation in Competition Law Enforcement, p. 15.

[3] OECD (2014): Challenges of International Co-operation in Competition Law Enforcement, p. 19.

F. I. Lessambo, *Mergers in the Global Markets*,
https://doi.org/10.1007/978-3-030-43558-5_7

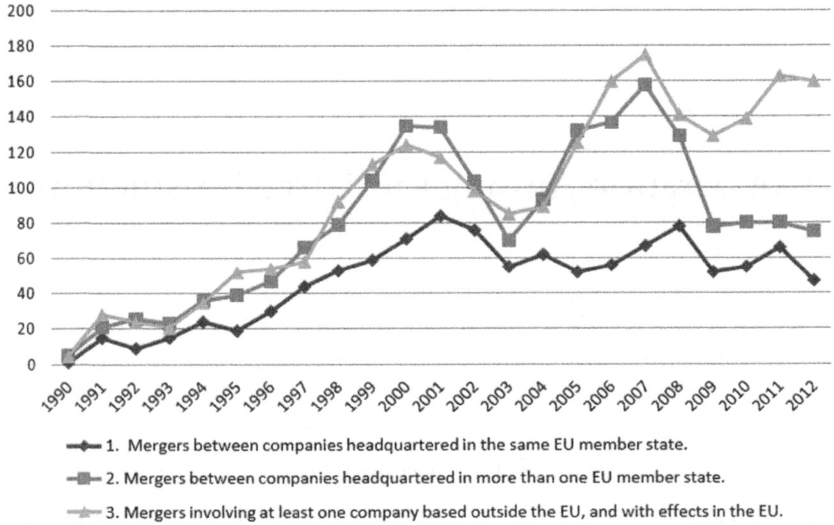

Fig. 7.1 Cross-border mergers (*Source* EU DG competition, OECD calculations)

7.2 Reasons of the Disagreements

By and large three main areas have been identified as sources of disagreement among the reviewing authorities: (i) differences in the pursued aims; (ii) differences in substantive rules; and (iii) differences in the assessment of the competition effects. In the EU, the Commission is the sole authority vested with the power to review merger. In the United States, both the DOJ and the FTC are vested with that authority. In China, more than five bodies are involved in the Merger review.

- The GE/Honeywell merger
  - GE is a behemoth manufacturing and services company based in Fairfield, Connecticut, with a reported $130 billion in revenues for 2000. It is one of the world's largest manufacturers of jet engines.
  - Honeywell, based in Morristown, New Jersey, reported $25 billion in sales for 2000. Honeywell is also a diversified manufacturing and technology company, involved in avionics products

and services, building and industrial controls, automotive products, power generation systems, specialty chemicals, fibers, and home security systems, among other things.

- On October 22, 2000, GE announced its proposed acquisition of Honeywell. The parties expected the deal to yield significant cost savings and considerable synergies in the aerospace industry.
- On May 3, 2001, the US Department of Justice ("DOJ") approved the proposed merger. The DOJ ruled that because the two companies had product ranges that were mostly complementary, the companies were not competitors. The DOJ requested that the parties undergo limited competitive concerns, specifically, that GE divest Honeywell's helicopter engine segment of business and license new competitors to maintain and repair certain Honeywell engines.
- On July 3, the Commission officially blocked the proposed merger. It concluded that the merger would create or strengthen dominant market positions in several markets and that the proposals made by GE were inadequate to resolve those competition concerns.
- The Commission was concerned that GE-Honeywell, due to efficiencies and economies of scale, could offer a combination of jet engines and avionics at lower prices. Commission stated that bundling would allow GE-Honeywell to induce customers to purchase GE-Honeywell products. This would increase their market share and cause "damaging profit shrinkage" for competitors.

7.3 International Anti-Trust Cooperation

7.3.1 Bilateral Cooperation

Cooperation enables the agencies to identify issues of common interest, improve our analyses, and avoid inconsistent outcomes.[4] In a bilateral agreement, states or jurisdictions would agree under which conditions

[4] Randolph Tritell and Elizabeth Kraus (2018): The Federal Trade Commission's International Antitrust Program, p. 4.

they would allow an execution of extraterritorial jurisdiction on their territory. Cooperation can either be a review cooperation or a remedies cooperation or both.

- The US bilateral cooperation

The US antitrust agencies cooperate with foreign competition agencies through formal and informal agreements and arrangements; cooperation also takes place without such agreements.[5] In 2017, the FTC cooperated on 38 mergers and anticompetitive conduct cases of mutual concern with counterpart agencies from 21 jurisdictions.[6] For instance, in reviewing the proposed Abbott/St. Jude merger,[7] the FTC agents cooperated with their counterparts from the antitrust agencies of Brazil, Canada, China, the European Union, Israel, Korea, and South Africa, including on the remedy and divestiture package to ensure an appropriate buyer for global assets. Likewise, in the investigation of ChemChina/Syngenta,[8] FTC agents worked with antitrust agencies of Australia, Canada, the European Union, India, and Mexico to exchange views about the competitive implications of the proposed transaction and coordinate reviews, and coordinated remedies with the European Commission and Mexico's COFECE.

- The EU bilateral cooperation

Cooperation aims to facilitate consistent outcomes in individual cases and convergence in relation to merger assessment principles in general. It also increases investigative efficiency by reducing duplication of work, delays, and burdens for the merging parties, third parties, and the agencies.[9] Such a cooperation between agencies is especially beneficial in cases

[5] Idem, p. 4.

[6] Idem, p. 5.

[7] https://www.ftc.gov/news-events/press-releases/2016/12/ftc-puts-conditions-abbott-laboratories-proposed-25-billion.

[8] https://www.ftc.gov/news-events/press-releases/2017/04/ftc-requires-china-national-chemical-corporationsyngenta-ag.

[9] EC (2016): International Enforcement Co-operation in Mergers: Main Principles and Recent Experiences, p. 1.

that raise competitive issues of common concern. This is particularly the case for mergers affecting global or cross-border regional markets. However, it may also be relevant where the geographic scope of the markets is confined to the respective jurisdictions.[10] The merging parties have a key role to play in facilitating cooperation between different agencies, in particular when cooperation requires aligning the timing of the review processes or the exchange of confidential information. Indeed the early and constructive engagement of merging parties is very important to successful interagency cooperation. By facilitating initial contacts and information sharing between agencies as well as timing alignment, the merging parties may facilitate information sharing by giving waivers of confidentiality (waivers). Waivers are therefore not a must-have for cooperation to be successful, and the Commission will ask for and make use of them in a responsible manner. For instance, in General Electric/Alstom,[11] the Commission cooperated closely with the US Department of Justice. The Commission and the US DOJ did, on the other hand, identify common concerns regarding the servicing of GE's mature gas turbines for 50 Hz and 60 Hz, where a subsidiary of Alstom was one of the very few capable independent service providers. Despite the different points of focus in the two agencies' assessments, close cooperation, in particular on the design of the remedies, led to satisfactory and mutually supportive remedy solutions for both the Commission's more far-reaching and the US DOJ's more limited concerns.[12] Cooperation in remedy design or/and remedy implementation is also vital. Cooperation in remedy design increases the likelihood of consistency in the scope or parameters of remedies accepted by different agencies. Likewise, remedy implementation cooperation provides more cost-efficient outcomes.[13] For instance, in UTC/Goodrich case,[14] the cooperation between the Commission and the US DOJ is extensive. Timing alignment and confidentiality waivers allowed not only for synergies for the agencies and the parties resulting from joint investigative efforts, but also coordination

[10] EC (2016): International Enforcement Co-operation in Mergers: Main Principles and Recent Experiences, p. 2.

[11] M.7278—Commission Decision of 8 September 2015.

[12] Idem.

[13] Idem, p. 5.

[14] M.6410—Commission Decision of 26 July 2012.

on remedy design, including the exchange of remedy proposals received from the parties and detailed discussions (involving the sharing of confidential information) on the design of remedies suitable to remedying the competition concerns. The agencies discussed the scope of divestment remedies, including the details and the duration of transitional arrangements between the merged entity and the divestment business, as well as key timelines for implementation of the remedies.[15]

Antitrust cooperation is highly active between the EU and the US agencies. Pursuant to the EU–US agreement of 1991 on antitrust cooperation, the European Commission examines any merger in parallel with the US Department of Justice. The two authorities conduct independent and separate investigations but the Commission and the US Department of Justice have enjoyed a good working relationship. The MCI/Sprint proposed merger illustrates the extent of the cooperation between the EU and the United States. The MCI WorldCom/Sprint merger proposal was notified, inter alia, to the Antitrust Division of the United States Department of Justice, and the European Commission. The parties granted appropriate waivers in order to enable the DOJ and the European Commission to exchange information and documents supplied by the parties to the two agencies. Many firms who responded to parallel enquiries from both the DOJ and the European Commission were prepared to let the two agencies exchange information, or supplied the same submission to both. In the course of the investigation and analysis of the merger proposal there was a considerable degree of cooperation between the two agencies, involving preliminary exchanges of views on the analytical framework, coordinated requests for information, attendance of DOJ observers at the oral hearing and joint meetings with the notifying parties. On May 15, 2000, the Director General for Competition sent a letter to the United States Assistant Attorney General requesting the cooperation of the DOJ in evaluating the impact of the merger on the US long-distance market and its consequences on the international telephony field. The key facts of the proposed merger can be summarized as follows:

[15] EC (2016): International Enforcement Co-operation in Mergers: Main Principles and Recent Experiences, p. 5.

- On January 11, 2000, the European Commission received notification of the proposed merger of the US telephone and Internet giants MCI and Sprint.
- MCI WorldCom is the world's leading provider of Internet connectivity, with Sprint one of its main competitors.
- MCI WorldCom provides a wide range of telecommunication services to businesses and consumers, including facilities-based local, long distance and international free phone, calling card, debit card and Internet services.
- Sprint provides in the USA local, long distance, and wireless communications and Internet services. Sprint's activities in Europe were (until Sprint's withdrawal from its participation in Global One, a joint venture with Deutsche Telekom and France Telecom) conducted through Global One.
- The parties argued before the FCC that the merger would have no impact on competition in which case, according to the two-tier approach, the Commission would have cleared the merger. However, the Federal Commission did not accept the argument as it consequently denied clearance.
- The undertakings concerned have a combined aggregate worldwide turnover of more than five billion Euros. Both MCI World and Sprint had a community-wide turnover in excess of EUR 250 million, but they do not achieve more than two-thirds of their aggregate community-wide turnover within one and the same Member State.
- On February 21, 2000, after examination of the notification, the European Commission concluded that the proposed commitment was not sufficient to remedy the competition concerns raised by the proposed transaction and accordingly the operation fell within the scope of the Merger Regulation and raised serious doubts as to its compatibility with the common market, and decided to initiate proceedings pursuant to Article 6(1)(c) of the Merger Regulation.
- On March 20, 2000, the European Commission required MCI WorldCom and Sprint to supply the outstanding information necessary to complete its investigation no later than March 24, 2000 at 08.00 CET.
- On June 27, 2000, the parties informed the Commission of their intention to formally withdraw the notification because they did not any longer propose to implement the proposed merger in the form presented in the notification. However, this did not amount to a

formal withdrawal of the merger agreement signed on October 4, 1999, that is the object of the notification. In addition, the parties left open the possibility for them to implement the proposed merger in a form different to the notification. For these reasons, the Commission could not accept such notice as a formal withdrawal of the transaction.

- An in-depth investigation by the Commission showed that the merger would, through the combination of the merging parties' extensive networks and large customer base, have led to the creation of such a powerful force that both competitors and customers would have been dependent on the new company to obtain universal internet connectivity.
- Put differently, this would have allowed the merged company to behave independently of both its competitors and customers and, therefore, to dictate conditions and prices in the market to the detriment of consumers around the world and particularly in the 15 European Union states.
- MCI WorldCom had a market share of 40–60% whereas Sprint, the second largest top-level network provider, had a share of 10–15%.
- Following the Commission's objections, the companies offered on June 8, 2000, to divest Sprint's Internet business from Sprint's other activities. However, the Commission's investigation showed that this proposal was insufficient as it would not reestablish, with enough certainty as to its effect, immediate and effective competition in the market for top-level internet connectivity.
- When assessing the feasibility of the proposed divestiture, the Commission also took into account issues raised by Cable & Wireless after its purchase of Internet MCI which was divested from MCI's other activities to gain clearance of the WorldCom/MCI merger in 1998.

> It was vital for the Commission that the divested business became a strong, viable competitor to prevent the merged WorldCom/Sprint from dominating Internet backbone. The companies' offer failed to guarantee this because Sprint's Internet business is completely intertwined with its traditional telecoms activities.

- The Commission also studied the impact of the merger in the market for the provision of global telecommunications services to multinational companies where together with British Telecommunications'

Concert alliance with AT&T the merged entity would appear to control the majority of the market.
- However, the Commission could not show the absence of competitive constraints from actual competitors in this market and that customers would not be able to countervail against any parallel behavior by the two leading players. Therefore, the Commission concluded that a collective dominant position could not be established between the merged entity and the Concert alliance.
- During the course of its investigation, the Commission also received a number of critical comments from US- and EU-based operators that the merger would lead to the creation of a joint dominant position in the international voice telephony market with AT&T on the U.S. retail and wholesale long distance market. The Commission's investigation showed that if there was any risk for competition in this market it would be a consequence of the exercise of market power on upstream domestic U.S. markets and that these effects in the EU would not be immediate or foreseeable enough to grant jurisdiction over this issue to the European Commission. The Commission therefore decided to draw the U.S. authorities' attention to these possible effects and to request them to take them into account in their investigation.

- China bilateral cooperation

China review authority under the AML, MOFCOM is also pursuing bilateral cooperation with several counterparts worldwide. MOFCOM has coordinated with enforcers in major jurisdictions such as the EU DG Com, the US FTC/DOJ, and South Korea's KFTC in several review processes.[16]

7.3.2 *The Exchange of Information*

The exchange of information among competition agencies is vital to insure stability in the global arena. On July 21, 2011, the US DOJ

[16]Thomas O. Barnett and Deborah Garza (2019): Competition Law Enforcement Trends in the US, EU, and China: Looking Ahead to 2018, *National Law Review*, p. 9.

and the FTC signed a memorandum of understanding with the Chinese antitrust agencies to promote communication and cooperation between the two countries. Likewise, under Article II of the Agreement between the United States and the European Union concerning the application of their competition laws, "Each Party shall notify the other whenever its competition authorities become aware that their enforcement activities may affect important interests of the other Party."[17] The two parties agree that it is in their common interest to share information that will (a) facilitate effective application of their respective competition laws, or (b) promote better understanding by them of economic conditions and theories relevant to their competition authorities' enforcement activities and interventions or participation of the kind described in Article II(5).[18]

7.3.3 *Enforcement of International Comity*

International comity is a prudential doctrine reflecting one sovereign's deference to another sovereign's acts and policies. Considerations of international comity often restrain courts from exercising jurisdiction over cases that might otherwise satisfy the effects test.[19] Comity is a choice-of-law principle that concerns the extent to which the law of one nation, as put in force within its territory, whether by executive order, by legislative act, or by judicial decree, shall be allowed to operate within the dominion of another nation.[20] Comity involves two aspects: first, a country's consideration of how it may prevent its law enforcement actions from

[17] OJ L 95, 27.4.1995, pp. 47–52 Approved by the decision of the Council and the Commission of 10 April 1995 (95/145/EC, ECSC).

[18] Article II (5) States: Each Party shall also notify the other whenever its competition authorities intervene or otherwise participate in a regulatory or judicial proceeding that does not arise from its enforcement activities, if the issues addressed in the intervention or participation may affect the other Party's important interests. Notification under this paragraph shall apply only to: (a) regulatory or judicial proceedings that are public; (b) intervention or participation that is public and pursuant to formal procedures; and (c) in the case of regulatory proceeding in the United States, only proceedings before federal agencies.

Notification shall be made at the time of the intervention or participation or as soon thereafter as possible.

[19] John Jay Jurata (2015): A New Trade War—Applying Domestic Antitrust Laws to Foreign Patents. *George Mason Law Review*, Vol. 22, No. 5, p. 1150.

[20] Hilton v. Guyot, 159 U.S. 113, 164 (1895).

harming another country's important interests, and second, a country's consideration of another country's request that it open or expand a law enforcement proceeding in order to remedy conduct that is substantially and adversely affecting that country's interest.

When determining whether to assert antitrust jurisdiction and bring an action in a particular case, the US Department of Justice and the Federal Trade Commission consider the following principles of international comity:

- the relative significance to the alleged violation of conduct within the United States, as compared to conduct abroad;
- the nationality of the persons involved in or affected by the conduct;
- the presence or absence of a purpose to affect U.S. consumers, markets, or exporters;
- the relative significance and foreseeability of the effects of the conduct on the United States as compared to the effects abroad;
- the existence of reasonable expectations that would be furthered or
- defeated by the action;
- the degree of conflict with foreign law or articulated foreign economic policies;
- the extent to which the enforcement activities of another country with respect to the same persons, including remedies resulting from those activities, may be affected; and
- the effectiveness of foreign enforcement as compared to U.S. enforcement action.

Recently, the U.S. Supreme Court, in Vitamin C ruling, analyzed the application of foreign laws in US courts.[21] The core facts of the litigation can be summed up as follows:

- U.S. purchasers of vitamin C filed a class action suit against four Chinese manufacturers who make the vitamin product in China and export it to the United States.
- The U.S. purchasers alleged that the Chinese manufacturers violated § 1 of the Sherman Act by operating as a cartel and agreeing to fix the price and quantity of the exports to the United States.

[21] Animal Sci. Products, Inc., v. Hebei Welcome Pharm. Co., 138 S. Ct. 1865 (2018).

- In their rebuttal, the Chinese manufacturers argued that their pricing regime was mandated by the Chinese Government and that they therefore were shielded from antitrust liability under state action doctrine, the foreign sovereign compulsion doctrine, and principles of international comity.
- Though the Chinese Ministry of Commerce (MOFCOM) submitted an amicus brief and a statement in support of defendants' arguments, the district court denied the Chinese manufacturers' motions to dismiss and for summary judgment.
- After a jury found for the U.S. purchasers and made an award of $147 million in damages, the Second Circuit reversed in 2016, holding that the district court erred by denying the motion to dismiss. The Second Circuit found that when a foreign government submits an official statement on the meaning and interpretation of its laws, federal courts are "bound to defer" to the foreign government's construction of its laws, whenever that construction is "reasonable."
- In the unanimous decision written by Justice Ginsburg, the Court found that when determining foreign law under FRCP 44.1, "[a] federal court should accord respectful consideration to a foreign government's submission, but *is not bound* to accord conclusive effect to the foreign government's statements."
- The Supreme Court reiterated Fed. R. Crim. P. 26.1's provision that in ascertaining foreign law, courts may consider "any relevant material or source" without regard to whether it is admissible under the Federal Rules of Evidence.
- The court concluded that the Second Circuit's "unyielding rule" was inappropriate and inconsistent with the broad approach of Rule 44.1.
- However, it should be noted that the Supreme Court did not undertake the comity analysis itself but remanded the case back to the Second Circuit Court of Appeals for renewed consideration consistent with its opinion.

7.4 The Search for an International Institution

7.4.1 *The OECD*

Founded in 1961, the Organization for Economic Co-operation and Development (OECD) is an intergovernmental economic organization with 36 member countries working in concert to stimulate economic progress and world trade.[22] Since its inception, the organization has played a vital role in international efforts to avoid international conflicts over the extraterritorial application of competition laws. Some have argued that, the OECD should be the best forum to provide guidelines to resolve international competition conflicts. The OECD has been involved in nonbinding recommendations in competition policy enforcement since the 1960s. With its long experience, expertise, not being a rulemaking organization, its efforts would be welcome by its members and beyond. Its Competition Committee provides a forum for senior representatives of members' competition agencies to exchange ideas and discuss policies of mutual interests. The primary goals of the Competition Committee consist of[23]:

(i) discussing the developments and identifying the best practices in competition law, policy, and enforcement;
(ii) fostering convergence among national antitrust policies; and
(iii) encouraging increased cooperation among antitrust agencies.

The Committee has developed nonbinding but important recommendations, including an antitrust enforcement cooperation, combating hardcore cartels, merger review procedures, and competition assessment.

7.4.2 *The WTO*

Founded in January, 2015, the World Trade Organization (WTO) is the only global international organization dealing with the rules of trade between nations.[24] Its goal is to ensure that trade flows as smoothly, predictably, and freely as possible.

[22] WWW.OECD.

[23] Randolph Tritell and Elizabeth Kraus (2018): The Federal Trade Commission's International Antitrust Program, p. 9.

[24] WWW.WTO.org.

The increasing interaction between trade and competition, including the so-called hybrid private/government restraints, has made the interface of competition regimes with trade regimes closer than any time before.

> The importance of competition policy for world trade is also manifested by the increasing incorporation of undertakings on competition policy in the Protocols of Accessions that apply to new WTO Members, and in the work of the WTO Trade Policy Review Body, which systematically references developments regarding national competition policies in developed and developing jurisdictions.[25]

On February 3, 1992, Sir Leon Brittan, then EU Commissioner on competition policy, proposed at the World Competition Forum at Davos to explore the possibility of making common rules on competition within the framework of the WTO. [26] Following the EU proposal, it was decided at the Singapore Ministerial meeting in 1996 to set up a working group in the WTO. Key WTO members (i.e., Japan and South Korea) have been favorable to the proposal. The European Union laid down the following arguments: (i) competition law enforcement is gaining an increasingly international dimension; (ii) the WTO objective of trade liberalization and a commitment to effective competition law enforcement are closely connected; and (iii) despite differences in domestic legal and institutional structures, there is growing international consensus regarding the fundamentals of competition law and policy. The United States, on the other hand, rejected the proposal of any WTO agreement at this stage, arguing that the WTO lacked substantial expertise on the subject matter.[27]

7.4.3 The UNCTDA

The United Nations Conference on Trade and Development (UNCTAD) holds meetings of Experts on Competition Law and Policy to monitor a voluntary international antitrust code of conduct adopted in 1980 by the U.N. General Assembly and to discuss competition law and policy generally.

[25] Robert D. Anderson, William E. Kovacic, Anna Caroline Müller, and Nadezhda Sporysheva (2018): Competition Policy, Trade and the Global Economy: Existing WTO Elements, Commitments in Regional Trade Agreements, Current Challenges and Issues for Reflection, World Trade Organization Economic Research and Statistics Division.

[26] Philip Marsden (2003): *A Competition Policy for the WTO*. London: Cameron May.

[27] Idem.

7.4.4 The International Competition Network

Created in October 2001, to increase understanding of competition policy and promote convergence toward sound antitrust enforcement around the world, the ICN, founded by 15 members including the FTC and the Department of Justice's Antitrust Division, has grown to 135 member agencies from 122 jurisdictions, supported by a wide network of nongovernmental advisors from around the world. The ICN serves as an important forum to further advance international coordination and cooperation of antitrust enforcement based on sound economics, procedural fairness, transparency and nondiscriminatory treatment of parties. The ICN is organized into working groups comprised of agencies and nongovernmental advisors. It plays a central role in promoting collaboration among antitrust authorities from around the world. It aims to promote convergence toward best practices in merger process and analysis and seeks to reduce the public and private costs of multijurisdictional merger reviews. At its annual meeting, in May 2017, the International Competition Network (ICN) adopted new recommended practices for merger review, addressing notification thresholds, remedies, and efficiencies; a framework for analyzing unilateral conduct; guiding principles for market studies; and a report on setting cartel fines. In 2019, the Merger Working Group presented a report on vertical mergers and promoted the use of its Framework for Merger Review Cooperation, developing explanatory material on the types of documents typically exchanged in multijurisdictional merger review to support sound enforcement cooperation. Overall, the adoption by numerous ICN members of key aspects of the Recommended Practices, such as merger thresholds that incorporate an appreciable nexus between the transaction and the jurisdiction, and objectively quantifiable notification thresholds, is widely viewed as a major accomplishment of the ICN that has improved the merger review process for merging parties and competition agencies.[28]

[28] Randolph Tritell and Elizabeth Kraus (2018): The Federal Trade Commission's International Antitrust Program, p. 9.

Glossary

Actual cost of debt means the interest rate the company was actually paying at the time of the merger

Cartel is formed when competitors make an agreement, an arrangement or conspire to lessen or prevent competition. The most common forms of cartel conduct include rigging bids, fixing prices, market allocation, and output restriction

Comity The legal principle that political entities (such as states, nations, or courts from different jurisdictions) will mutually recognize each other's legislative, executive, and judicial acts

Conglomerate merger is a merger between firms that are involved in totally unrelated business activities. These mergers typically occur between firms within different industries or firms located in different geographical locations

Extraterritoriality The effect of remedies on the international antitrust system. Under the Clayton Act, *mergers* and acquisitions involving parties outside the United States are similarly subject to the jurisdiction of U.S. law

Fair value [in the context of an appraisal proceeding] is the value to a stockholder of the firm as a going concern, as opposed to the firm's value in the context of an acquisition or other transaction

Foreign direct investment is defined as the purchase of real assets abroad for the purpose of acquiring a lasting interest in an enterprise and exerting a degree of influence on that enterprise's operations

F. I. Lessambo, *Mergers in the Global Markets*,
https://doi.org/10.1007/978-3-030-43558-5

Gun-jumping refers to a variety of actions that merging parties might enter into prior to closing to facilitate the merger and expedite the integration of the companies

The Herfindahl–Hirschman Index is a measure of market concentration that squares the market shares of all the firms in a market, and then sums them. It ranges from 0 (perfect competition) to 10,000 (pure monopoly). According to the Horizontal Merger Guidelines, the threshold for a "highly concentrated" market is above 2500. The HHI examines the relationship between the number of competitors and their respective market share in order to determine how concentrated a market is and what change in the index will occur through a merger. The HHI is calculated by summing the squares of the market shares of each firm in the market

Horizontal merger is a *merger* or business consolidation that occurs between firms that operate in the same industry

Hostile takeover is the acquisition of one company (called the target company) by another (called the acquirer) that is accomplished by going directly to the company's shareholders or fighting to replace management to get the acquisition approved

Mergers and acquisitions A merger is a business event wherein two or more companies decide to pool their assets to form a single new company. In the course of this transaction, one of the previously existing companies ceases to exist. An acquisition does not necessarily constitute a merger if the preexisting companies continue to exist

Monopoly is a business entity that has significant market power, that is, the power to charge overly high prices

Monopsony is sometimes used to refer to a wide range of harms that result from a powerful buyer or a reduction in competition among buyers

Negative control addresses situations in which a person or entity obtains an explicit veto right through contract or through a level of share ownership or board representation at a level that does not amount to majority control, but nevertheless is sufficient to block certain actions that may require, for example, a supermajority vote

Proxy Put a provision that may be included in a company's credit agreements requiring the company to refinance its debt in the event of a change in the majority of the board, if that change was not approved by a majority of the preexisting directors

Rogatory letter is a request from a judge in the United States to the judiciary of a foreign country requesting the performance of an act, which, if done without the sanction of the foreign court, would constitute a violation of that country's sovereignty

Standstill obligation is a contract that contains provisions that govern how a bidder of a company can purchase, dispose of, or vote stock of the target company

Strategic partnerships A strategic partnership is a formal alliance (joint venture, licensing agreement, distributorship, or agency contract) between two commercial enterprises, usually formalized by one or more business contracts, where they mutually participate in certain activities (advertising, branding, product development, etc.)

Vertical merger is the *merger* of two or more companies involved at different stages in the supply chain process for a common good or service. Most often, the *merger* is purposed to increase synergies, gain more control of the supply chain process, and increase business

Bibliography

Alford, Roger P. (1992): The Extraterritorial Application of Antitrust Laws: The United States and European Community Approaches, *Virginia Journal of International Law*, Vol. 33, pp. 6–7.

Baker, Donald I., and John DeQ Briggs (2004): Rethinking U.S. Antitrust Policy and Administration: Joining the Rest of the World in the 21st Century, *Loyola Consumer Law Review*, Vol. 379, p. 4.

Barnett, O. Thomas, and Deborah Garza (2019): Competition Law Enforcement Trends in the US, EU, and China: Looking Ahead to 2018, *National Law Review*, p. 9.

Basedoq, Jurgen (2007): The Modernization of European Competition Law: A Story of Unfinished Concepts, *Texas International Law Review*, Vol. 42:429, p. 435.

Bath, Vivienne (2013): National Security and Chinese Investment Policy, *Harvard Business Law Review* (online), Vol. 3, p. 85.

Beckler, Richard W. (2003): Extraterritorial Application of U.S. Antitrust Law: What Is a "Direct, Substantial, and Reasonably Foreseeable Effect" Under the Foreign Trade Antitrust Improvements Act? *Texas International Law Review*, Vol. 38:11, p. 19.

Buccirossi, Paolo, and Lorenzo Ciari (2011): Competition Policy and Productivity Growth: An Empirical Assessment, Düsseldorf Institute for Competition Economics (DICE), p. 24.

Chin, Yee Wah (2012): M&A under China's Anti-Monopoly Laws, Victoria University of Wellington Law School.

F. I. Lessambo, *Mergers in the Global Markets*,
https://doi.org/10.1007/978-3-030-43558-5

Council Regulation 139/2004 of 20 January 2004 on the Control of Concentrations Between Undertakings, 2004 O.J. (L 24) 1 (EC) [hereinafter EC Merger Regulation].

Dea, Destiny D. (2008): The Costs of Perceived Hypocrisy: The Impact of US Treatment of Foreign Acquisitions of Domestic Enterprises, *Duke Law Review*, Vol. 57:1795, p. 1801.

Ezrachi, Ariel (2015): Sponge, The University of Oxford Centre for Competition Law and Policy, Working Paper CCLP (L) 42, p. 8.

Farmer, Susan Beth (2010): The Impact of China's Antitrust Law and Other Competition Policies on US Companies, *Loyola Consumer Law Review*, Vol. 23:1, p. 36.

Foroohar, Rana (2014): Why Big Mergers Are Bad for Consumers, time.com, July 31.

Gates, Michael (2016): Cross-Cultural Issues Relating to the DaimlerChrysler Merge—Case Study.

Hao, Zhan, Song Yin, and Stephanie Wu (2019): Global Legal Insights, Cartel 2019-China.

Jurata, John J. (2015): A New Trade War—Applying Domestic Antitrust Laws to Foreign Patents. *George Mason Law Review*, Vol. 22:5, p. 1150.

Kiriaziz, Georgios (2001): Jurisdiction and Cooperation Issues in the Investigation of International Cartels, DG COMP-A-4, p. 1.

Kovacic, William E. (2007): The Intellectual DNA of Modern U.S. Competition Law for Dominant Firm Conduct: The Chicago/Harvard Double Helix, *Columbia Business Law Review*, Vol. 1, pp. 6–7.

Kwoka, John (2017): The Structural Presumption and the Safe Harbor in Merger Review: False Positives or Unwarranted Concerns? *Antitrust Law Journal*, Vol. 81, p. 841.

Lewis, Jeffrey I.D. (2014): What Is "FRAND" All About? The Licensing of Patents Essential to an Accepted Standard, *Cardozo Law Review*.

Liu, Cheng, Audrey Yumeng Li, and Jeff Liu (2019): Navigating Through Merger Control Review in China—Challenges for U.S. Companies During a Time of Uncertainty, https://www.competitionpolicyinternational.com.

Majoras, Deborah P. (2001): GE-Honeywell: The US Decision, Antitrust Law Section State Bar of Georgia, p. 3.

Mao, Zhang (2018): Devoted to Promoting Innovation and Reform in Market Regulation, available at http://samr.saic.gov.cn/xw/yw/zj/201805/t20180502_274005.html.

Minjian, You (2010): To Understand Abuse of Market Dominance in Anti-Monopoly Law, Chinaipmagazine.com.

MOFCOM Announcement [2011] No. 33 regarding the Anti-Monopoly Review Decision for Conditional Clearance of the Combination of Joint Stock Company Uralkali with Joint Stock Company Silvinit, http://fldj.mofcom.gov.cn/

aarticle/zcfb/201106/20110607583288.html (in Chinese) (visited February 17, 2012).
Monti, Mario (2001): European Competition for the 21st Century, *Fordham International Law Journal*, Vol. 24, pp. 1602, 1604.
Mozur, Paul (2016): Obama Moves to Block Chinese Acquisition of a German Chip Maker, *New York Times*, December 12, 2016.
OECD (2012): Competition Policy: Promoting Efficiency and Sound Market.
OECD (2012): The Role of Efficiency Claims in Antitrust Proceedings.
OECD (2014): Challenges of International Co-operation in Competition Law Enforcement, p. 35.
OECD (2014): Factsheet on How Competition Policy Affects Macro-Economic Outcomes, p. 14.
Orbach, Barak (2013): How Antitrust Lost Its Goal, *Fordham Law review*, Vol. 81:5, p. 2254.
Scott Hemphill, C., and Nancy L. Rose (2018): Mergers That Harm Sellers, *The Yale Law Journal*, Vol. 127, p. 2091.
Shapiro, Carl (2019): Protecting Competition in the American Economy: Merger Control, Tech Titans, Labor Markets, *Journal of Economic Perspectives*, Vol. 33:3, Summer 2019, p. 70.
Shi, Lin (2009): Research on the Efficiency of China's Anti-Monopoly Law, *Asian Social Science*, Vol. 5, p. 97.
Smith, William F. (1982): Changing Enforcement Policy, *Antitrust Law Journal*, Vol. 51, pp. 95, 101.
Steinbaum, Marshall, and Maurice E. Stuke (2018): The Effective Competition Standards, The Roosevelt Institute, pp. 8–9.
Teachout, Zephyr (2018): Mega-mergers like AT&T and Time Warner Crush American Democracy, *The Guardian*.
Thomas, Daniel (2015): Are Big Mergers Bad for Consumers? Business Reporter, October 30.
Tritell, Randolph, and Elizabeth Kraus (2018): The Federal Trade Commission's International Antitrust Program.
United States Government Accountability Office (July 2008): Foreign Investment: Laws and Policies Regulating Foreign Investment in 10 Countries, pp. 42–43.
U.S. Department of Justice and Federal Trade Communication, Horizontal Merger Guidelines (hereinafter Merger Guidelines) § 10 (2010), available at http://www.justice.gov/atr/public/guidelines/hmg-2010.pdf.
Velve, Lawrence R. (1976): Carving Holes in the Sherman Act: A Comment on the Citizens & Southern Case, *Catholic University Law Review*, Vol. 25, p. 543.

Yu, Huang Xian (2015): Huiyuan's Acquisition by Coca-Cola in PRC—Case Analysis, *Journal of Economics, Business and Management*, Vol. 3:2, February 2015, p. 271.

Zephyr Annual M&A Activity Report Global, FY 2015, p. 3.

Zucker, Jeremy B., and Sven Schulte-Hillen (2016): Following CFIUS Recommendation, President Obama Blocks Chinese Acquisition of US-German Semiconductor Equipment Manufacturer, Dechert LLP, December 20, 2016.

Index

F. I. Lessambo, *Mergers in the Global Markets*,
https://doi.org/10.1007/978-3-030-43558-5

The manufacturer's authorised representative in the EU is Springer Nature Customer Service Centre GmbH, Europaplatz 3, 69115 Heidelberg, Germany. If you have any concerns regarding our products, please contact ProductSafety@springernature.com

Printed and bound by CPI Group (UK) Ltd, Croydon, CR0 4YY
30/09/2026
02225459-0001